OUR DESTINY

THE CALL AND ELECTION OF THE HOUSE OF ISRAEL

OUR DESTINY

THE CALL AND ELECTION OF THE HOUSE OF ISRAEL

ROBERT L. MILLET
JOSEPH FIELDING McCONKIE

BOOKCRAFT
Salt Lake City, Utah

This book is a private endeavor and is not an official publication of either The Church of Jesus Christ of Latter-day Saints or Brigham Young University.

Copyright © 1993 by Bookcraft, Inc.

All rights reserved. No part of this book may be reproduced in any form or by any means without permission in writing from the publisher, Bookcraft, Inc., 1848 West 2300 South, Salt Lake City, Utah 84119.

Bookcraft is a registered trademark of Bookcraft, Inc.

Library of Congress Catalog Card Number: 93–72101
ISBN 0–88494–888–9

2nd Printing, 1994

Printed in the United States of America

Let this then be our covenant—whatever the past has been—let this then be our covenant, that we will walk in all the ordinances of the Lord blameless. Let this be our covenant, that we will keep the commandments of God and be living witnesses of the truth and divinity of this glorious work, which is destined to sweep the earth as with a flood and which shall cover the earth as the waters cover the sea.

O God, grant that I and my family and all the faithful members of the house of Israel may walk in truth and light, and having enjoyed the fellowship and kinship and association that is found nowhere else on earth outside the Church, let us enjoy that same spirit, that same fellowship in its eternal fullness, in the mansions and realms which are ahead.

Bruce R. McConkie
Solemn Assembly, 6 October 1972

Contents

	Acknowledgments	ix
	Prologue	1
1	A Lost Doctrine	5
2	Israel Before the World Was	15
3	An Everlasting Covenant	29
4	The History of Histories	39
5	The Morning Breaks, the Shadows Flee	51
6	The Scattering and Gathering of Israel	65
7	A Covenant People in Ancient America	85
8	A Scriptural Search for the Ten Tribes	103
9	The Place of the Covenant	119
10	Millennial Israel: One Fold and One Shepherd	129
	Epilogue	141
	Bibliography	145
	Index	149

Acknowledgments

We are pleased to acknowledge the painstaking research efforts of Philip L. Allred. His careful study, over many months, of ancient and modern records of both Latter-day Saint and non-Latter-day Saint sources has proven extremely helpful in the preparation of this work.

We also express gratitude to Lori Soza, a conscientious and capable secretary and assistant, for her efforts in bringing this book through rough drafts to published form.

Prologue

A doctrine that remains untaught is a doctrine ignored. Like an unplanted seed, it bears no fruit and gives no nourishment. When God planted earth's most beautiful and perfect garden eastward in Eden, he not only planted that which would "please the eye" and "gladden the heart" but also that which would be good for "food and for raiment, for taste and for smell, to strengthen the body and to enliven the soul" (D&C 59:17–18). Of necessity, Adam and Eve had to be familiar with all such plants, in preparation for the day when they would be required to provide for themselves and for their family.

It was a lone and dreary world into which they came when they were driven from their primeval home, but surely it would not have remained so for long. Eve, with her recent vision of paradise, would have beautified it with all manner of flowers and plants. Yet one does not eat flowers, and it would have been necessary for them to cultivate both fruits and vegetables. How grateful they must have been for that experience in Eden where God had taught them how to dress and keep a garden!

So it would be also with the seeds of their spiritual understanding, for they came not to earth to labor for their temporal salvation but rather for that which is eternal. Their knowledge of the gospel, the perfection of their understanding, would of necessity have to embrace more than that which pleased the eye and gladdened the heart, for their souls would demand nourishment. Simply put, the gospel of Jesus Christ must embrace more than just those doctrines that all find immediately pleasing. Christianity cannot be reduced to the flowers of love and kindness alone. They are an enriching part of the gospel, but they do not carry with them the source of nourishment and strength that enables us to accomplish the arduous tasks of the day.

The essence of Christianity is Christ—the truths associated with his divine sonship and his atoning sacrifice. As God's Son, he and he alone could atone for the sins of mankind. He could make it possible for all who so desired to return to the presence of their Eternal Father. Not only is he our Savior—he is also our Lord and Master. "We believe that through the Atonement of Christ, all mankind may be saved, by obedience to the laws and ordinances of the Gospel" (Articles of Faith 1:3). He bought us with a price, and it is his right to require our obedience to principles of righteousness and truth. Salvation is obtained only on his terms. It is not negotiable. A meaningful understanding of the gospel will not reduce paradise to a flower garden or the ministry of Christ to the virtues of the Scout Law. Such were not the reasons that Christ suffered an infinite agony at Gethsemane and Calvary.

According to holy writ, whenever the Lord has a people that he acknowledges as his own, that acknowledgment comes in the form of a covenant. In our day we hear much about "making a commitment for Christ." It is *covenants* of which we should speak, not commitments. The word *commitment* is not found in the scriptures. The word *covenant* is found a multitude of times. A commitment is a personal pledge and may even be quite serious, while, scripturally speaking, a covenant is a two-way promise and is always sacred. God is its author and the guarantor of its terms. Angels are its witnesses. In the realm of eternal things, a covenant is a legal and binding agreement between God and an individual or group of people.

Attendant to the doctrine of a covenant people is the concept of a chosen people. Just as the Lord's people are always a covenant people, so it can be said that they are also always a chosen people—a people who claim both a special calling and an election. In so saying, we are keenly aware that the idea of a covenant or chosen people is not a particularly popular or fashionable doctrine in our egalitarian age. It is nevertheless an eternal part of the gospel plan. To suppose that it is but a loose thread that can be pulled from the fabric of the gospel cloth would be to make the mistake of unraveling the entirety of holy writ and the entirety of the gospel plan.

In his dedicatory prayer for the Kirtland Temple, Joseph Smith asked the Lord to "put upon" his "servants the testimony of the covenant" (D&C 109:38). That plea catches the spirit of a chosen people. It identifies that they have been chosen not as royalty but as servants who, according to the covenant made with father Abraham, must bear the message of salvation to all the nations of the earth. It is for others to amass the wealth of the earth and to be crowned with the honors and plaudits of men. It is for Israel, the Lord's chosen, to be their servants, ministering to their spiritual needs. Given that the purity of the gospel cannot be preserved nor conveyed in impure vessels, it becomes the lot of Israel to be in the world and yet not of it. "I pray not that thou shouldest take them out of the world," Jesus prayed on the night before his crucifixion, "but that thou shouldest keep them from the evil. They are not of the world, even as I am not of the world. Sanctify them through thy truth: thy word is truth. As thou hast sent me into the world, even so have I also sent them into the world. And for their sakes I sanctify myself, that they also might be sanctified through the truth." (John 17:15–19.)

How strange it is that there are those who would not think of eating food prepared in an unclean kitchen or delivered by a soiled waiter yet at the same time suppose that the sacred fruits of everlasting life can be treated with less care. Can we in soberness, even for one moment, suppose that one of impure and unsanctified hands and heart can stand in the stead of the Holy One of Israel to teach the truths of salvation and perform his ordinances? Has not the divine decree always been "Be ye clean, that bear the vessels of the Lord"? (Isaiah 52:11; D&C 133:5.) There are those who will desire to eat from the table of the Lord, and there must be a people prepared to minister to their desires save they perish.

As a people, we Latter-day Saints suffer with a spiritual schizophrenia, desiring on the one hand not to be thought of as supposing ourselves different or more loved of God than any others, and yet anxious on the other hand to be true to our birthright as a people—a people called and set apart at a special time for a special purpose. But our calling requires that we seek to echo the prayer of the Prophet: "[Lord,] put upon thy servants the testimony of the covenant." Our destiny as a people is to make a difference in this world, something that we can do only if we are willing to be different.

1

A Lost Doctrine

*They have taken away from the gospel of the Lamb many parts
which are plain and most precious; and also many covenants
of the Lord have they taken away.*
—1 Nephi 13:26

Prophesying of key events that would precipitate the great night of darkness—the universal apostasy that followed the ministry of Christ—Nephi spoke of a great and abominable church that would take "away from the gospel of the Lamb many parts which are plain and most precious"; and, he added, "many covenants of the Lord have they taken away" (1 Nephi 13:26). Only then, after it had been tampered with, would the book that we know as the Holy Bible go forth among the children of men and throughout the nations of the earth. Because of those plain and precious things that were taken from the book, Nephi said, an "exceedingly great many" would stumble, and Satan would have "great power over them" (1 Nephi 13:29).

An Evil Victory

These excisions made in scriptural records were more than pious fraud. They were the seal on the work of those who destroyed the meridian Church. The perpetrators labored from within. In tampering with the writings of the Apostles and prophets, they sought to ensure their dynasty of darkness, and in that regard they were, as Nephi prophesied, largely successful.

Despite what many within the Church suppose, the great difficulty that we as Latter-day Saints have with the Bible is not alone a matter of translation errors. There are problems with matters of translation, to be sure, but it must be recognized that there are sufficient men with adequate scholarly tools in virtually every denomination of any moment to ensure that no one is going to go too far astray with faulty translations. The great issue described by Nephi is not translation, but *transmission*. The purity of the texts translated is the issue. A perfectly correct translation of a faulty document will always be faulty. In his preface to the revelation on the degrees of glory, Joseph Smith wrote, "From sundry revelations which had been received, it was apparent that many important points touching the salvation of man, had been taken from the Bible, or lost before it was compiled" (*History of the Church*, 1:245).

The plain, the precious, and the covenants of the Lord were the things taken. Who did it, when they did it, and how they did it are questions to which we do not now have complete answers. However, that someone did it is amply evident by the revelations of the Restoration. The Book of Mormon and the revelations given to the Prophet Joseph Smith, along with the restoration of the priesthood and its keys, clearly attest to this. That an "exceedingly great many" have stumbled and continue to stumble because of that which is missing from the Bible is also abundantly evident. The Protestant world alone, while professing loyalty to the Bible, has divided itself into thousands of different denominations. Truth seekers often find themselves lost in the war of words and tumult of opinions spoken of by Joseph Smith as he sought to determine which church to join. Of that experience he said, "The teachers of religion of the different sects understood the same passages of scripture so differently as to destroy all confidence in settling the question by an appeal to the Bible" (Joseph Smith—History 1:12). The Bible simply does not have the kind of clarity common to the revelations of the Restoration. Some scholars even delight in its ambiguity.

Latter-day Saints often mistakenly suppose when people of other faiths ask theological questions that we should answer them from the Bible, supposing it to be common ground. In fact, it is not. There is little consensus on any biblical issue, be it the nature of the Bible's origin, its authority, or matters of interpretation. In fact, agreement cannot even be found on what books belong in the Bible—the Jews have a Bible that embraces what we know as the Old Testament, the Protestants add some twenty-seven books known to us as the New Testament, while the Roman Catholics add from the intertestamental period another fifteen books commonly called the Old Testament Apocrypha. They are all using editions containing differences that arise from their having come from different families of manuscripts.

The range of "precious" things taken from the Bible reaches from the small to the great and back again. For instance, oceans of ink have been spilt by Bible commentators attempting to explain the meaning of Christ's reference to himself as the "son of man." Who is his father—Joseph or God? Or is he simply a mortal manifestation of the Father, as announced in many Christian creeds? How precious and yet simple is the answer when we learn that he is the "Son of Man," meaning, of course, "Son of Man of Holiness" (Moses 6:57). His Father is an exalted, glorified man in whose image we were literally created.

And what became of the written testimony of John the Baptist? Modern revelation promises a future day when it will be restored to us in its fulness (D&C 93:18). Such promises also include the full account of the experience of Peter, James, and John on the Mount of Transfiguration (D&C 63:20–21) and such historical and doctrinal details as the following event in the life of the Master: "Then said the Pharisees unto him, Why will ye not receive us with our baptism, seeing we keep the whole law? But Jesus said unto them, Ye keep not the law. If ye had kept the law, ye would have received me, for I am he who gave the law. I receive not you with your baptism, because it profiteth you nothing. For when that which is new is come, the old is ready to be put away." (JST Matthew 9:18–21.)

Scores of illustrations could be cited of the plain and the precious truths that have been lost to this marvelous book. Our attention, however, is centered on the concept of covenants, for the Lord's people have always been a covenant people. To take from the people of God a knowledge of those covenants would be to take that which in the system of teaching the gospel is most plain and most precious—the ordinances and promises of salvation. To lose such knowledge is to lose both root and branch, to lose one's spiritual moorings, to be driven with the wind and tossed, to be as a man without a country, without a family, and without a destiny. Without this knowledge our lives are, as Malachi said, cursed (see Malachi 4:5–6), or as Moroni put it, "utterly wasted" (D&C 2:3). Such has been the adversary's victory during the long night of apostate darkness.

Principles That Build upon Each Other

In the context of the Bible, whenever the Lord had a people that he acknowledged as his own, that acknowledgment came in the form of a covenant relationship. Simply stated, the Lord's people were a covenant people, and standing at their head was a prophet or covenant spokesman. Their system of worship centered around the temple, the place of the covenant and the place of revelation. Without revelation there can be no covenant, for a covenant requires mutual consent. It has no silent partners.

To administer the covenant also requires priesthood, the authority to act for God. This again sustains the need for revelation, for without revelation there can be no priesthood. Indeed, "the question might be asked," wrote Oliver Cowdery, "have men authority to administer in the name of Christ, who deny revelations, when His testimony is no less than the spirit of prophecy, and His religion based, built, and sustained by immediate revelations, in all ages of the world when He has had a people on earth?" (Footnote to Joseph Smith—History 1:71.)

The covenant and its promised blessings centered in and around the family, for salvation is a family affair. The promise given to Abraham and repeated to Isaac and Jacob was that of posterity as numberless as the stars of heaven or the sands upon the seashore (see D&C 132:30). Again when Jacob gave Joseph a father's blessing, his paramount promise was that he would be "a fruitful bough," blessed with the "blessings of the breasts, and of the womb" (Genesis 49:22, 25). Later, Joseph would say to his brethren, "The Lord hath visited me, and I have obtained a promise of the Lord, that out of the fruit of my loins, the Lord God will raise up a righteous branch out of my loins" (JST Genesis 50:24). Abraham was also assured that the promises relative to his posterity would not be dissolved by death: "Both in the world and out of the world," he was assured, they would continue

(D&C 132:30). This would be accomplished through what we know as the crowning ordinance of the gospel, identified in latter-day revelation as the new and everlasting covenant of marriage (see D&C 131:2).

Among the Lord's ancient covenant people, salvation was a family affair, not an individual matter. The joys of life beyond the grave were depicted as a great family reunion. Abraham was assured that in death he would go to his fathers in peace (see Genesis 15:15), that he would be "gathered to his people" (Genesis 25:8). Similarly, Joseph of Egypt in his old age gathered his family around him and said, "I die, and go unto my fathers; and I go down to my grave with joy" (JST Genesis 50:24). So inseparable was the idea of family and paradise that Christ denominated this place of the faithful departed spirits as "Abraham's bosom" (Luke 16:22).

These doctrines—covenants, temples, living prophets, immediate revelation, priesthood, eternal marriage, and the continuation of the family unit—are all jewels on the crown of exaltation. They belong together, and they glorify each other. When the knowledge of one is lost, then the knowledge of the others is lost in short order. In like manner, in this dispensation of the fulness of times when the covenant of salvation was restored to the Prophet Joseph Smith, the other jewels of salvation were restored, each in their natural order. The family of true doctrine is sealed together.

We Stand Alone

In our day, apart from Latter-day Saints, there are few in the Bible-believing world who even profess to be a covenant people or who would see any particular need for or relevance in such a claim. Among those professing a covenant relationship with God, the nature of that relationship is sharply different from that known to those of Bible times. Virtually no one is claiming the existence of prophets or covenant spokesmen in the Bible pattern. The Christian and Jewish worlds speak with a united voice in announcing the canon of scripture complete. They profess revelation only in the sense of "fresh encounters with sacred texts," but all would regard it as heresy to suppose that someone today could ascend Sinai and come back with a written revelation that not only had a rightful place in the canon of extant scripture but could edit or supersede it, as did the revelations of Moses and Christ, the classic covenant spokesmen of the Old and New Testaments.

Aside from some "fundamentalist" offshoots, whose claims fail on several grounds, no one outside The Church of Jesus Christ of Latter-day Saints makes claim to the power and authority to perform marriages that are eternal and to create family units that are endless, as was the case with Abraham, Isaac, and Jacob. As Latter-day Saints we stand alone. The visible symbol of our uniqueness is our temples—the place of the covenant. The covenant of which we speak is known to us as the new and everlasting covenant. It is new only in the sense of its restoration in our day, for unlike the evolving doctrines of the rest of the world, its principles are everlastingly the same. It is not rooted in tradition. As in ancient times, it professes direct revelation as its source. We have it at the hands of God and angels.

The Covenant

This loss of the knowledge of the covenant finds expression in the titles we have given the two divisions within the Bible. What we know as the Old and New Testaments could more properly be called the Old and New Covenants. It is recorded that at the Last Supper, while Christ and his Apostles were seated around what might be called the sacrament table, Jesus said: "This is my blood of the new testament, which is shed for many for the remission of sins" (Matthew 26:28). A more appropriate rendering of this might be "for this signifies my 'blood of the covenant.' "

Though the words *testament* and *covenant* share common ground, the idea of a covenant is certainly more expressive. The emphasis shifts from that of a witness to that of a sacred obligation. As teachers of the New Testament (the New Covenant), we (the authors) must make a decision as to whether we are teaching a course on the content of four books that are descriptive of events in the life and ministry of Jesus or whether we will place the emphasis of the course on actually teaching the new covenant introduced by Christ. Is it the knowledge of religious history that is our primary objective in teaching, or is it the knowledge of an eternal covenant?

The Gospel of Mark, which many believe to be the first of the

Gospels written, introduces its narrative with an account of Jesus' baptism. Is it not significant that the story of the New Covenant begin with an account of Jesus, who is referred to prophetically as "the messenger of the covenant" (Malachi 3:1), entering into a new covenant? It will be remembered that John was reluctant to baptize the Savior, feeling himself unworthy even to unlatch his shoes. "Suffer it to be so now," the Savior insisted, "for thus it becometh us to fulfil all righteousness" (Matthew 3:15). Righteousness requires obedience. The eternal order of heaven demanded that Christ be immersed in the waters of baptism at the hands of John so that they together might fulfill all righteousness. Nephi, writing by the spirit of revelation, explained how in the waters of baptism the Son of God complied with the demands of the law. First, he said, Christ humbled himself before the Father; second, he witnessed "unto the Father that he would be obedient unto him in keeping his commandments" (his part of the covenant); and third, he showed "unto the children of men the straitness of the path, and the narrowness of the gate, by which they [must] enter" the divine presence (2 Nephi 31:5–9). And finally, as Elder Bruce R. McConkie has stated in commentary on the Nephite text, "Though he is the King of the kingdom, though he authors and proclaims his Father's plan of salvation, though he ordains and establishes the laws governing all things, yet he cannot enter the kingdom of heaven without baptism" (*The Mortal Messiah* 1:402). Thus it was that the Messenger of the covenant complied with the message.

John the Baptist's role was to prepare the way for the Lord. He did so, in part at least, through the ordinance of baptism. Such was his practice in the meridian of time, and such was the authority that he restored in the fulness of times. "I confer the Priesthood of Aaron," the Baptist said to Joseph and Oliver, "which holds the keys of the ministering of angels, and of the gospel of repentance, and of baptism by immersion for the remission of sins" (D&C 13:1). He whose role it was to "make straight the way of the Lord" (John 1:23; Isaiah 40:3) did so through the medium of a covenant.

In the first chapter of John we read of a delegation of priests and Levites from the temple being sent down to Bethabara to investigate John the Baptist. John was asked if he was the Messiah. He answered that he was not. He was asked if he was Elias (meaning Elijah), and he said, "No." He was asked if he was "that prophet" (obviously a prophet of restoration whose prophesied coming was well known to the Jews of Jesus' day—see JST Matthew 17:14). Again, he said that he was not. "Why baptizest thou then, if thou be not that Christ, nor Elias, neither that prophet?" he was asked. The question is more significant than John's answer. It illustrates that the Jews of Jesus' day knew that all true servants of the Lord come baptizing. They expected the Messiah to come baptizing, they expected Elijah who had been translated and taken into heaven to come baptizing, and they expected the mighty prophet of the Restoration, who was very much a part of their messianic tradition, to come baptizing.

Surely it is significant that when we compare the Sermon on the Mount as found in Matthew with its counterpart in 3 Nephi, one of the singular differences we find is that in the New World account of this discourse baptism is added to the list of beatitudes (see 3 Nephi 12:1–2). This changes the flavor of everything that follows. The sermon can no longer be viewed as the instruction of a great ethical teacher in the community but must be understood as the Messiah announcing the covenant of salvation. This is a classic example of the plain and precious truths, even the covenants of the Lord, being taken from the Bible text as Nephi had prophesied.

The new and everlasting covenant, which is the fulness of the gospel, embraces "all covenants, contracts, bonds, obligations, oaths, vows, performances, connections, associations, or expectations" that are to be of "efficacy, virtue, or force in and after the resurrection from the dead" (D&C 132:7). Yet, the new and everlasting covenant that must precede all others is the ordinance of baptism. This explains why the resurrected Christ in his first meeting with the Nephites at the temple in Bountiful gave Nephi and the others of the Twelve the authority to baptize all of their nation anew. Baptism had been faithfully practiced by the Nephites for over six hundred years, but now a new dispensation was being introduced. The old covenant had been fulfilled and it was time to introduce the new. Well might Christ have said to the nation of the Nephites as he did to the faithful of our own day:

> Behold, I say unto you that all old covenants have I caused to be done away in this thing; and this is a new and an everlasting covenant, even that which was from the beginning.
> Wherefore, although a man should be baptized an hundred times it availeth him nothing, for you cannot enter in at the strait gate by the law of Moses, neither by your dead works.

For it is because of your dead works that I have caused this last covenant and this church to be built up unto me, even as in days of old.

Wherefore, enter ye in at the gate, as I have commanded, and seek not to counsel your God. (D&C 22:1–4.)

The Breadth of the Doctrine

Sometimes we mistakenly suppose that because the restoration of the gospel formally began with the Church's organization in 1830, the apostasy ended at the same time. The first ray of light does not chase away the darkness of night; it simply stands as a harbinger of more light to come. At the present time many aspects of the apostasy are alive and well. They hold sway in every sphere of mortal activity that does not enjoy the full influence of gospel light. So it is with the scattering of Israel: it did not end at the moment that the great labor of the gathering began. The remnant of Jacob is at this very moment of time still being scattered.

Similarly, the assault on the concept of a covenant people has not ended. Like all other aspects of the apostasy, it is alive and well. In various shades of darkness it creeps into the thinking of the Latter-day Saint people. We need to be reminded that should we as a people lose either our understanding of the covenant God made with our ancient fathers or our faith in its application and relevance today, then we will lose with it its train of attendants—revelation, prophets, priesthood, and temple blessings. Such is the lesson of history.

Conclusion

As far as mortality is concerned, the idea that salvation is the fruit of sacred covenants has its earliest roots in the Garden of Eden. Be it remembered that Adam and Eve were not expelled from their Edenic state until they had entered into covenant with God and until they had been clothed in garments that symbolized the promise of their eventual redemption from their fallen state through the atoning blood of Christ (see Moses 4:27; 5:4–8). Yet, in the broader sense, the doctrine that salvation centers in covenants reaches to a time long before we were born. It has been named the new and everlasting covenant, thus emphasizing that though we enter into it anew in mortality and though it has been restored anew in this dispensation, its principles are everlasting and were known to us and agreed upon by us long before we were born into mortality. Emphasizing this very point, the Savior asked: "Will I appoint unto you, saith the Lord, except it be by law, even as I and my Father ordained unto you, before the world was?" (D&C 132:11.)

2

Israel Before the World Was

Now the Lord had shown unto me, Abraham, the intelligences that were organized before the world was; and among all these there were many of the noble and great ones.
—Abraham 3:22

One of the most settling but stimulating doctrinal concepts restored through the Prophet Joseph Smith is the idea that men and women lived before they were born into this life. The doctrine is so logical, so consistent, so theologically true to what people feel about life that many of those who investigate the Church find themselves saying, "Yes, I think I've always believed that." It is a vital part of life's puzzle. In short, as Elder Boyd K. Packer has observed, "There is no way to make sense out of life without a knowledge of the doctrine of premortal life. The idea that mortal birth is the beginning is preposterous. There is no way to explain life if you believe that . . . When we understand the doctrine of premortal life, then things fit together and make sense." (Conference Report, October 1983, p. 22.)

Organization in the First Estate

As with the individual, so also with persons and nations. Just as it is inconceivable that one person tabernacles the flesh at a given place and in a given time by chance alone (see Acts 17:26), so when it came to the organization of mankind into lineages and families nothing was left to chance. Our Father in Heaven is a God of order, and his house is a house of order. There is purpose and design in all he seeks to do, in all he seeks to bring to pass. Joseph Smith taught that there was an organization of the sons and daughters of God that took place in our premortal existence (see *Teachings of the Prophet Joseph Smith*, pp. 158, 181; cited hereafter as *Teachings*). This is borne out in a translation of an ancient text: "Now the Lord had shown unto me, Abraham, the intelligences that were organized before the world was; and among all these there were many of the noble and great ones" (Abraham 3:22). This refers not to their spirit birth, which would have taken place long before this time, but rather to their calling and election to certain blessings and responsibilities in the second estate. After his death the Prophet Joseph appeared to Brigham Young and pleaded: "Tell the people to be humble and faithful, and be sure to keep the Spirit of the Lord and it will lead them right. . . . Tell the brethren if they will follow the Spirit of the Lord, they will go right. Be sure to tell the people to keep the Spirit of the Lord; and if they will *they will find themselves just as they were organized by our Father in Heaven before they came into the world. Our Father in Heaven organized the human family*, but they are [now] all disorganized and in great confusion." (*Journal History*, 23 February 1847, emphasis added; cited in McConkie and Millet, *The Holy Ghost*, pp. 10–11.)

Following our birth as spirit sons and daughters of God, and being endowed with agency, we grew and developed and progressed according to our desires for truth and righteousness. It is customary to remark that in our first estate we walked by sight, while in this life we walk by faith. This is only partially true. In that pristine existence we walked by sight, and we walked by faith. The scriptures teach that some exercised exceedingly great faith and performed many good works (see Alma 13:3). That the Lord should state that many were among the noble and great ones certainly implies a gradation of faithfulness, that some were less noble and some even ignoble. "Being subject to law, and having their agency, all the spirits of men, while yet in the Eternal Presence, developed aptitudes, talents, capacities, and abilities of every sort, kind, and degree," Elder Bruce R. McConkie wrote.

During the long expanse of life which then was, an infinite variety of talents and abilities came into being. As the ages rolled on, no two spirits remained alike. Mozart became a musician; Einstein centered his interests in mathematics; Michaelangelo turned his attention to painting. Cain was a liar, a schemer, a rebel who maintained a close affinity to Lucifer. Abraham and Moses and all of the prophets sought and obtained the talent for spirituality. Mary and Eve were two of the greatest of all the spirit daughters of the Father. The whole house of Israel, known and segregated out from their fellows, was inclined toward spiritual things. And so it went through all the hosts of heaven, each individual developing such talents and abilities as his soul desired. (*The Mortal Messiah* 1:23.)

Though most often the Saints are prone to speak at length of individual foreordination to positions, callings, or assignments in the Church, perhaps the greatest foreordination or election, based on premortal faithfulness, is foreordination to lineage and family. Certain individuals come to earth through a designated channel, through a lineage that entitles them to specified blessings but also a lineage that carries with it burdens and responsibilities. This entails what our colleague Brent Top calls "a type of collective foreordination—a selection of spirits to form an entire favored group or lineage." Yet, he adds, "although it is a collective foreordination it is nonetheless based on individual premortal faithfulness and spiritual capacity." (*The Life Before*, p. 144.) In the words of Elder Melvin J. Ballard, Israel is "a group of souls tested, tried, and proven before they were born into the world. . . . Through this lineage were to come the true and tried souls that had demonstrated their righteousness in the spirit world before they came here." ("The Three Degrees of Glory," in *Melvin J. Ballard: Crusader for Righteousness*, pp. 218–19.)

"Remember the days of old," Moses counseled his people; "consider the years of many generations: ask thy father, and he will shew thee: thy elders, and they will tell thee. When the most High divided to the nations their inheritance, when he separated the sons of Adam, he set the bounds of the people according to the number of the children of Israel. For the Lord's portion is his people; Jacob is the lot of his inheritance." (Deuteronomy 32:7–9.) In speaking to the Athenians, the Apostle Paul declared: "God that made the world and all things therein . . . hath made of one blood all nations of men for to dwell on all the face of the earth, and hath determined the times before appointed, and the bounds of their habitation" (Acts 17:24, 26). President Harold B. Lee explained that

> those born to the lineage of Jacob, who was later to be called Israel, and his posterity, who were known as the children of Israel, were born into the most illustrious lineage of any of those who came upon the earth as mortal beings.
>
> All these rewards were seemingly promised, or foreordained, before the world was. Surely these matters must have been determined by the kind of lives we had lived in that premortal spirit world. Some may question these assumptions, but at the same time they will accept without any question the belief that each one of us will be judged when we leave this earth according to his or her deeds during our lives here in mortality. Isn't it just as reasonable to believe that what we have received here in this earth [life] was given to each of us according to the merits of our conduct before we came here? (Conference Report, October 1973, pp. 7–8.)

It thus appears that the declaration of our lineage by patriarchs is as much a statement about who and what we *were* as it is about who we are now and what we may become. There are those, of course, who believe otherwise, who believe that premortality has little or nothing to do with mortality, that there is no tie between faithfulness there and lineage and station here; to believe in any other way, they contend, is racist, sexist, or exclusivist. Despite the egalitarian-sounding nature of such a perspective, such views are doctrinally defenseless and even potentially hazardous. If there is no relationship between the first estate and the second, why, as President Lee might ask, should we believe there is any relationship between what we do here and what we will receive hereafter? Our task as parents and teachers and students of the gospel is not simply to win friends and influence people through avoiding, watering down, or in some cases even denying what are "hard sayings" or difficult doctrines. Truth is our guide and goal, and truth is not established by consensus or by popularity.

Who are we, then? President Lee answered: "You are all the sons and daughters of God."

> Your spirits were created and lived as organized intelligences before the world was. You have been blessed to have a physical body because of

your obedience to certain commandments in that premortal state. You are now born into a family to which you have come, into the nations through which you have come, as a reward for the kind of lives you lived before you came here and at a time in the world's history, as the Apostle Paul taught the men of Athens and as the Lord revealed to Moses, determined by the faithfulness of each of those who lived before this world was created. (Conference Report, October 1973, p. 7.)

The Burden of the Blessing

Is there some practical advantage to being a member of the house of Israel? Is there some notable blessing associated with lineage or family? For one thing, as we have indicated, we come to earth with differing capacities, many of which were developed in an earlier estate. "As it is with the prophets," Elder McConkie wrote, "so it is with all the chosen seed. 'God's elect,' as Paul calls them (Romans 8:33), are especially endowed at birth with spiritual talents. It is easier for them to believe the gospel than it is for the generality of mankind. Every living soul comes into this world with sufficient talent to believe and be saved, but the Lord's sheep, as a reward for their devotion when they dwelt in his presence, enjoy greater spiritual endowments than their fellows. To draw upon a phrase that the early Brethren frequently used, those of Israel come to earth with "believing blood," meaning that "those born in that lineage have both the right and a special spiritual capacity to recognize, receive, and believe the truth. The term is simply a beautiful, a poetic, and a symbolic way of referring to the seed of Abraham to whom the promises were made." (*A New Witness for the Articles of Faith,* p. 39; cited hereafter as *New Witness.*)

It was perhaps in this vein that Joseph Smith spoke of the impact of the Spirit of God upon the descendants of Abraham:

> [The] Holy Ghost has no other effect than pure intelligence. It is more powerful in expanding the mind, enlightening the understanding, and storing the intellect with present knowledge, of a man who is of the literal seed of Abraham, than one that is a Gentile, though it may not have half as much visible effect upon the body; for as the Holy Ghost falls upon one of the literal seed of Abraham, it is calm and serene; and his whole soul and body are only exercised by the pure spirit of

intelligence; while the effect of the Holy Ghost upon a Gentile, is to purge out the old blood, and make him actually of the seed of Abraham. (*Teachings*, pp. 149–50.)

Further, subject to their maintaining a righteous life in mortality, the people of Israel have a right, by lineage, to the blessings of the gospel, the priesthood, and ultimately to eternal life (see Abraham 2:8–11). The Lord operates through families, and he dispenses the blessings of the new and everlasting covenant through a covenant people, those spirits who by lineage and through personal righteousness are worthy of being known as the posterity of Abraham.

In writing poetically of the "Council of the Gods," in which Jehovah was appointed as the chief advocate and proponent of the Father's plan, Elder Orson F. Whitney has the Savior speak these words:

> Give me to lead to this lorn world,
> When wandered from the fold,
> Twelve legions of the noble ones
> That now thy face behold;
> Tried souls, 'mid untried spirits found;
> That captained these may be,
> And crowned the dispensations all
> With powers of Deity.

The Father grants the Redeemer's request and adds:

> After and ere thy going down,
> An army shall descend—
> The host of God, and house of him
> Whom I have named my friend.
> Through him, upon Idumea,
> Shall come, all life to leaven,
> The guileless ones, the sovereign sons,
> Throned on the heights of heaven.
> (As cited in *Seeking After Our Dead: Our Greatest Responsibility*, p. 23.)

As Elder Whitney's poem implies, coming to earth through a peculiar lineage involves more than boasting of a blessing. It involves much more than gloating over one's premortal chosenness; it entails bearing a burden. Israel has been sent to earth to serve as a leavening influence. Indeed, God has called Israel to be a light to the nations (see Isaiah 49:6). More specifically, as a part of God's covenant with Abraham, Deity has decreed that the gospel and the blessings of the priesthood are to be administered through Abraham's descendants. Elder Parley P. Pratt spoke of Israel's election (and her duty) in the flesh:

> We read much in the Bible in relation to a choice or *election*, on the part of Deity, towards intelligences in His government on earth, whereby some were chosen to fill stations very different from others. And this election not only affected the individuals thus chosen, but their posterity for long generations. . . .
> It may be inquired where this election first originated, and upon what principle a just and impartial God exercises the elective franchise. We will go back to the earliest knowledge we have of the existence of intelligences. . . .
> Among the intelligences [i.e., "organized intelligences" or spirits] which existed in the beginning, some were more intelligent than others, or, in other words, more noble; and God said to Abraham, "These I will make my rulers!" God said unto Abraham, "Thou art one of them; thou wast chosen before thou wast born." . . .
> . . . When He [God] speaks of nobility, He simply means an election made, and an office or a title conferred, on the principle of superiority of intellect, or nobleness of action, or of capacity to act. And when this election, with its titles, dignities, and estates, includes the unborn posterity of a chosen man, as in the case of Abraham, Isaac, and Jacob, it is with a view of the noble spirits of the eternal world coming through their lineage, and being taught in the commandments of God. Hence the Prophets, Kings, Priests, Patriarchs, Apostles, and even Jesus Christ, were included in the election of Abraham, and of his seed, as manifested to him in an eternal covenant.

Thus it is, Elder Pratt continued, that "in this peculiar lineage, and in no other, should all the nations be blessed. From the days of Abraham until now, if the people of any country, age, or nation, have been blessed with the blessings peculiar to the everlasting covenant of the Gospel, its sealing powers, Priesthood, and ordinances, it has been through the ministry of that lineage, and the keys of Priesthood held by the lawful heirs according to the flesh." (*Journal of Discourses* 1:257–58, 261; cited hereafter as *JD*.)

A chosen people are called upon to make choices that evidence their covenant with Christ and their loyalty to the fathers. A chosen people are called upon to be true to their covenants. Israel is called to live the gospel. Israel is called to share the gospel. Israel is called to be the light to a world that travels largely in darkness. Years ago a wise man wrote of the burdens of chosenness and of why God has selected a particular people as his own:

> A man may rise and demand, "By what right does God choose one race or people above another?" I like that form of the question. It is much better than asking by what right God degrades one people beneath another, although that is implied. God's grading is always upward. If He raises up a nation, it is that other nations may be raised up through its ministry. If He exalts a great man, an apostle of liberty or science or faith, it is that He might raise a degraded people to a better condition. The divine selection is not [alone] a prize, a compliment paid to the man or the race—it is a burden imposed. To appoint a Chosen people is not a pandering to the racial vanity of a "superior people," it is a yoke bound upon the necks of those who are chosen for a special service.

In short, "the Lord hath made [Israel] great for what He is going to make [Israel] do." (W. J. Cameron, "Is There a Chosen People?" in James H. Anderson, *God's Covenant Race*, pp. 300–2.)

Covenants Made Before We Were Born

Having declared that his house is a house of order and not a house of confusion, the Lord asked: "Will I appoint unto you . . . except it be by law, even as I and my Father ordained unto you, before the world was?" (D&C 132:11.) The Apostle Paul spoke of the gospel as the hope that is laid up for us in heaven, "whereof ye heard before in the word of the truth" of it (Colossians 1:5). That is to say, gospel principles were taught to us and understood by us long before we were born. Building on that understanding, Elder Lorenzo Snow said: "Had we not kept what is called our first estate and observed the laws that governed there, you and I would not be here today. We are here because we are worthy to be here, and that arises, to a great extent at least, from the fact that we kept our first estate. I believe that when you and I were in yonder life we made certain covenants with those that had the control, that in this life, when we should be permitted to enter it, we would do what we had done in that life—find out the will of God and conform to it." (*Deseret Weekly*, 12 May 1894, 48:637.)

President Spencer W. Kimball, referring to the pre-earth life, said: "Here you and I made . . . an oath that we would do all things whatsoever the Lord our God shall command us. While we do not remember the details, we made these covenants. We committed ourselves to our Heavenly Father that if he would send us to earth and give us bodies and give to us the priceless opportunities that earth life afforded, we would keep our lives clean and would marry in the holy temple and rear a family and teach them righteousness. This was a solemn oath, a solemn promise, an eternal commitment." ("Be Ye Therefore Perfect," address given at the Institute of Religion at the University of Utah, 10 January 1975.)

A proper understanding of the doctrine of agency is dependent also upon understanding this concept of pre-earth covenants. President Joseph Fielding Smith illustrated this, saying:

> I have heard people say, and members of the Church too, "I have a right to do as I please." My answer is: No, you do not. You haven't any right at all to do just as you please. There is only one right that you have, and that is to . . . keep the commandments of Jesus Christ. He has a perfect right to tell us so. We have no right to refuse. I do not care who the man is; I do not care where he lives, or what he is—when the gospel of Jesus Christ is presented to him, he has no right to refuse to receive it. He has the privilege. He is not compelled to receive it, because our Father in heaven has given to everyone of us, in the Church and out, the gift of free agency. That free agency gives us the privilege to accept and be loyal to our Lord's commandments, but it has never given us the right to reject them. Every man who rejects the commandments of our Father in heaven is rebellious. (Conference Report, April 1967, pp. 120–21.)

The whole system of declaring the gospel to the nations of the earth rests on the reality of a pre-earth life, the covenants we made there, and the understanding that we bring with us into mortality. We do not send missionaries out simply to declare God's existence. We assume that people know and believe in him. We do so because we know that all men are born with the Light of Christ (see D&C 84:46;

93:2). To one degree or another, they are born with a testimony of eternal truths. We do not go out into the world to argue gospel truths; we go out to proclaim them. In doing so, we expect the honest in heart to recognize and respond to them. Thus we find the Savior saying: "My sheep hear my voice, and I know them, and they follow me" (John 10:27). That is, they innately and naturally respond to principles of truth and to the spirit of truth. The great majority of people who join the Church tell us they knew the message was true from the moment we began to teach them.

When Moroni appeared to Joseph Smith in 1823, he quoted a prophecy, made by Malachi, with some variation from the way we have it in our King James Bible. He said that Elijah would "plant in the hearts of the children the promises made to the fathers" (D&C 2:2; Joseph Smith—History 1:39). In our premortal life we no doubt made promises, to God and to those who went before but had no opportunity to enjoy gospel privileges, that we would do our part to see to it that the ordinances of salvation were made available to them. Again, it is the duty of the members of the house of Israel to be ministers of the gospel of salvation. Elder John A. Widtsoe thus observed that "in our preexistent state . . . we made a certain agreement with the Almighty. The Lord proposed a plan. . . . We accepted it." He continued:

> Since the plan is intended for all men, we became parties to the salvation of every person under that plan. We agreed, right then and there, to be not only saviors for ourselves, but . . . saviors for the whole human family. We went into a partnership with the Lord. The working out of the plan became then not merely the Father's work, and the Savior's work, but also our work. The least of us, the humblest, is in partnership with the Almighty in achieving the purpose of the eternal plan of salvation.
>
> That places us in a very responsible attitude towards the human race. By that doctrine, with the Lord at the head, we become saviors on Mount Zion, all committed to the great plan of offering salvation to the untold numbers of spirits. To do this is the Lord's self-imposed duty, this great labor his greatest glory. Likewise, it is man's duty, self-imposed, his pleasure and joy, his labor, and ultimately his glory. (*The Utah Genealogical and Historical Magazine*, October 1934, vol. 25, p. 189.)

Many Called, Few Chosen

Premortal faithfulness is not sufficient to guarantee salvation. Nor is the fact that one's patriarchal blessing signifies Abrahamic descent enough to ensure exaltation in the highest heaven hereafter. The desires and talents and attributes we developed in our first estate must be realized and find a meaningful place in our lives here in this second estate. Likewise, our descent through a chosen lineage must be matched by noble and careful choices, choices that demonstrate our covenant consciousness. Alma taught that some of those who exercised exceedingly great faith in their premortal existence fail to do the same in this life; they harden their hearts and blind their minds to those spiritual impressions that ever whisper of our former standing and our ultimate possibilities (see Alma 13:4–5). They were then called and elected and foreordained to greatness, all on a conditional basis. When those conditions, however, are not met—when the children of promise yield to the persuasions of this sphere and thus succumb to the allurements of a fallen world—the transcendent promises that might have been theirs slip away. President Harold B. Lee warned:

> Despite that calling which is spoken of in the scriptures as "foreordination," we have another inspired declaration: "Behold, there are many called, but few are chosen. . . ." (D&C 121:34.)
>
> This suggests that even though we have our free agency here, there are many who were foreordained before the world was, to a greater state than they have prepared themselves for here. Even though they might have been among the noble and great, from among whom the Father declared he would make his chosen leaders, they may fail of that calling here in mortality. (Conference Report, October 1973, p. 7.)

In the same way, being blessed to be of the tribe of Ephraim or of Manasseh or of Judah does not guarantee an elect status either here or hereafter. Jesus and John the Baptist constantly sought to raise the sights of those in the meridian of time whose pride and haughtiness lay in their lineage.

> The Baptist scolded: O, generation of vipers, who hath warned you to flee from the wrath to come?

> Why is it that ye receive not the preaching of him whom God hath sent? If ye receive not this in your hearts, ye receive not me; and if ye receive not me, ye receive not him of whom I am sent to bear record; and for your sins ye have no cloak.
> Repent, therefore, and bring forth fruits meet for repentance;
> And think not to say within yourselves, We are the children of Abraham, and we only have power to bring seed unto our father Abraham; for I say unto you that God is able of these stones to raise up children into Abraham. (JST Matthew 3:33–36.)

Indeed, God does not delight in arrogance or feelings of lineal superiority. The Almighty was and is able to raise up seed unto Abraham, even through those "stony Gentiles" whom so many of the Jews of that day resented and snubbed (see *Teachings*, p. 319).

The Master himself condemned those whose preoccupation with genealogy precluded their properly perceiving their place in God's plan. He uttered a timeless truth when he said, "If ye were Abraham's children, ye would do the works of Abraham" (John 8:39). That is to say, "If you were truly descendants of Abraham, you would come unto the Lord of Life as did the Father of the Faithful. You would be willing to lay down your all in sacrifice of the things of this world to truly come to know God. More specifically, you would recognize and acknowledge who I am, delight in my doctrine, open yourselves to my truths, and be saved through my redemption." In short, many of the Jews of Jesus' day broke their covenants through rejecting the Living Oracle, even he who was the Mediator of the New Covenant.

> We be Abraham's children, the Jews said to Jove;
> We shall follow our Father, inherit his trove.
> But from Jesus our Lord, came the stinging rebuke:
> Ye are children of him, whom ye list to obey;
> Were ye Abraham's seed, ye would walk in his path,
> And escape the strong chains of the father of wrath.
>
> We have Moses the seer, and the prophets of old;
> All their words we shall treasure as silver and gold.
> But from Jesus our Lord, came the sobering voice:
> If to Moses ye turn, then give heed to his word;
> Only then can ye hope for rewards of great worth,
> For he spake of my coming and labors on earth.

> We have Peter and Paul, in their steps let us trod;
> So religionists say, as they worship their God.
> But speaks He who is Lord of the living and dead:
> In the hands of those prophets, those teachers and seers,
> Who abide in your day have I given the keys;
> Unto them ye must turn, the Eternal to please.
> (Bruce R. McConkie, Conference Report, April 1974, pp. 100–101.)

Truly, as Paul says: "They are not all Israel, which are of Israel: Neither, because they are all children of Abraham, are they the seed" (JST Romans 9:6–7). Only those who are the seed of Christ—who have hearkened to the voice of the Lord's servants, have put on Christ, and have taken his name upon them (see Mosiah 15:10–12)—are truly the seed of Abraham. Such are covenant people. In a warning to latter-day Israel, Nephi declared:

> I, Nephi, would not suffer that ye should suppose that ye are more righteous than the Gentiles shall be. For behold, except ye shall keep the commandments of God ye shall all likewise perish; and because of the words which have been spoken [concerning the glorious destiny of the house of Israel] ye need not suppose that the Gentiles are utterly destroyed.
>
> For behold, I say unto you that as many of the Gentiles as will repent are the covenant people of the Lord; and as many of the Jews as will not repent shall be cast off; for the Lord covenanteth with none save it be with them that repent and believe in his Son, who is the Holy One of Israel. (2 Nephi 30:1–2.)

Conclusion

The time frame outlined by Zenos's allegory of the olive tree draws to a close as the millennial day witnesses the gathering of Israel in great numbers by the chosen servants and as the Gentiles join with Israel to constitute one royal family. "And thus they labored, with all diligence, according to the commandments of the Lord of the vineyard, even until the bad had been cast away out of the vineyard, and the Lord had preserved unto himself that the trees had become again the natural fruit; and they became like unto one body; and the fruits were equal; and the Lord of the vineyard had preserved unto himself the natural fruit, which was most precious unto him from the beginning" (Jacob 5:74). Truly Israel was, is, and will forevermore be precious to the Holy One of Israel. From Joseph Smith to Christ, from Christ to Abraham, and from Abraham to the foundations of the world, God has loved his chosen people. "Once we know who we are," Elder Russell M. Nelson said, "and the royal lineage of which we are a part, our actions and directions in life will be more appropriate to our inheritance" ("Thanks for the Covenant," *1988–89 Brigham Young University Devotional and Fireside Speeches*, p. 59).

3

An Everlasting Covenant

Ye are the salt of the earth: but if the salt have lost his savour, wherewith shall it be salted? it is thenceforth good for nothing, but to be cast out, and to be trodden under foot of men.
—Matthew 5:13

You have surely heard the expression, "He is not worth his salt." Have you wondered where it came from? In ancient times salt, which was often hard to obtain, was sufficiently valuable that it could be used as payment for services rendered. For example, in some instances it was used as part of a soldier's pay. Thus, to say that someone was not worth his salt was to say that he had not earned his wages.

A Salt Covenant

Today salt has more than 14,000 uses. It occupies an important place in all of our lives. In fact, we cannot live without it. Body cells must have salt in order to function. Despite salt's many modern uses, biblical peoples valued it much more highly than we do today. Anciently the newborn baby started out its life with a salt bath (see Ezekiel 16:4). Apparently this was to cleanse the child of impurities. Salt has antiseptic or germ-killing properties. Among some this salt bath was thought to help ward off evil spirits. In those dispensations in which the Lord's people practiced animal sacrifice, salt was sprinkled over the offering to purify it. Salt was also used to preserve the meat. Thus salt was a natural symbol for both purity and perpetuity. It was a symbol of incorruption and of a covenant that was to be everlasting. The scriptural expression for an enduring covenant became "a covenant of salt" (Numbers 18:19; 2 Chronicles 13:5). Even today the people of the Bible lands think of salt as a sign of honor, friendship, and hospitality. Arabs say, "There is salt between us," meaning, "We have eaten together and are friends." Singularly, the Arabs use the same word for salt that they do for a compact or a treaty.

This is the cultural background for the Savior's statement to his newly called Apostles in the Sermon on the Mount and to those assembled at the temple in Bountiful in the New World: "Ye are the salt of the earth: but if the salt have lost his savour, wherewith shall it be salted? it is thenceforth good for nothing, but to be cast out, and to be trodden under foot of men" (Matthew 5:13; compare 3 Nephi 12:13). In both instances, the Savior is addressing a covenant people. In fact, were we to refer to these discourses by their content rather than the place where they were delivered, we could call them the "Covenant Discourses." In these two sermons the imagery associated with salt makes it a perfect metaphor for the covenant that the Lord's people have made. As salt is essential to the life and health of the body, so covenants are essential to spiritual life and health. As salt purified and preserved the meat of sacrifice, so covenants purify the substance of our labors and renew or preserve our sacred promises.

Salt that has lost its savor, we are told, is good for nothing but to be cast out and trodden under foot. Salt does not dissipate with age; it carries no expiration date. Savor is lost through mixture and contamination—only diluting it with impure substances can cause it to lose its capacity to bless lives. As we would suppose, in ancient times salt was acquired in its natural state. It had to be washed before it could be used to season food or for other purposes. After it had been cleansed, the tailings or residue remained. This was tossed upon the walkways to be trodden down by the feet of men. How powerful the imagery! Once we have been gathered, we are washed and cleansed and the impure residue discarded. Our purpose then is to serve as a savor, to bring out the best, to elicit all that is good. This is a power lost to us only if we choose to contaminate ourselves with things of bad taste.

Born Under the Covenant

The restoration of the gospel is synonymous with a restoration of the Abrahamic covenant. That covenant contains the promise of continual revelation to Abraham's seed forever (see Luke 1:54–55). It also contains the promise of a fulness of gospel blessings. It is the promise to father Abraham that his seed will be heirs to the same covenants, knowledge, power, and priesthood by which he obtained his exaltation. No legitimate claim can be made to possessing the gospel of Jesus Christ without at the same time possessing all the blessings promised to Abraham's seed. Singularly, the Book of Mormon, which lays the theological foundations of Mormonism, begins with the announcement on the title page that its two most important theological themes and purposes are: first, to make known the covenant made to the fathers; and second, to bear testimony that Jesus is the Christ, the Eternal God. Moroni, the guardian of the record and its final contributor, explains on the title page that the Book of Mormon's purpose is "to show unto the remnant of the House of Israel what great things the Lord hath done for their fathers; and that they may know the covenants of the Lord, that they are not cast off forever—and also to the convincing of the Jew and Gentile that JESUS is the CHRIST, the ETERNAL GOD."

Even as we testify that there is no salvation independent of the knowledge that Jesus is the Christ, so we declare that there is no salvation independent of the knowledge of the covenant God made with Abraham—including its terms and conditions. The most perfect account of this covenant is preserved for us in a revelation written by the hand of Abraham:

> I will make of thee a great nation, and I will bless thee above measure, and make thy name great among all nations, and thou shalt be a blessing unto thy seed after thee, that in their hands they shall bear this ministry and Priesthood unto all nations;
>
> And I will bless them through thy name; for as many as receive this Gospel shall be called after thy name, and shall be accounted thy seed, and shall rise up and bless thee, as their father;
>
> And I will bless them that bless thee, and curse them that curse thee; and in thee (that is, in thy Priesthood) and in thy seed (that is, thy Priesthood), for I give unto thee a promise that this right shall continue in thee, and in thy seed after thee (that is to say, the literal seed, or the

seed of the body) shall all the families of the earth be blessed, even with the blessings of the Gospel, which are the blessings of salvation, even of life eternal (Abraham 2:9–11).

From this we learn that Abraham had the fulness of the gospel and the fulness of the priesthood, and that his seed would also enjoy the promise given him. Further, he was assured that because those blessings would be theirs, the responsibility would also be theirs to take the message of the gospel to the ends of the earth. All who were to receive the gospel from that point forward were to receive it at the hands of Abraham's seed. Those who had prepared themselves in the councils of heaven and had been true and faithful to the Father's plan and purposes were destined to be born into the family of Abraham, having claim to the promise given to their ancient father.

Those special promises granted Abraham were given anew to his son Isaac (see Genesis 26:1–5) and his grandson Jacob (see Genesis 28:3–4,10–15). Jacob in turn served as the Lord's mouthpiece in passing those blessings on to his twelve sons, who stood at the head of the twelve tribes of Israel. Joseph, who became the birthright son because of Reuben's transgression, was given a double blessing that was placed on the head of his two sons, Manasseh and Ephraim. In the Joseph Smith Translation, this part of the blessing is restored to us:

> For thou [Joseph] hast prevailed, and thy father's house hath bowed down unto thee, even as it was shown unto thee, before thou wast sold into Egypt by the hands of thy brethren; wherefore thy brethren shall bow down unto thee, from generation to generation, unto the fruit of thy loins for ever;
>
> For thou shall be a light unto my people, to deliver them in the days of their captivity, from bondage; and to bring salvation unto them, when they are altogether bowed down under sin (JST Genesis 48:10–11).

This is one of many passages that could be cited to show that the birthright would in the last days rest with Joseph's posterity. That is to say, by virtue of their birth they would have claim on the same gospel known to their fathers—Abraham, Isaac, and Jacob—and on the same priesthood with all its majesty and power. How is such heavenly favoritism justified? Because they prepared themselves, long before they were born, to carry that gospel with its attendant blessings to all nations and peoples of the earth. An indication of this is found in President Joseph F. Smith's great vision of the redemption of the dead. Witnessing in vision the world of spirits, President Smith said:

> The Prophet Joseph Smith, and my father, Hyrum Smith, Brigham Young, John Taylor, Wilford Woodruff, and other choice spirits who were reserved to come forth in the fulness of times to take part in laying the foundations of the great latter-day work,
> Including the building of the temples and the performance of ordinances therein for the redemption of the dead, were also in the spirit world.
> I observed that they were also among the noble and great ones who were chosen in the beginning to be rulers in the Church of God.
> Even before they were born, they, with many others, received their first lessons in the world of spirits and were prepared to come forth in the due time of the Lord to labor in his vineyard for the salvation of the souls of men. (D&C 138:53–56.)

The prophets named illustrate the principle. What is true of them is true of all the faithful Saints. The Lord once said, "What I say unto one I say unto all" (D&C 93:49). The revelations mention prophets as examples of the principle because their names are recognizable to us, but the principles involved are as true of every faithful Latter-day Saint as they are of our leaders. We have claim to being numbered among the "many others" referred to in this vision.

Thus it is that one of the great revelations describing the events of the last days records that those of the other tribes of Israel will eventually return and fall down to be crowned with glory at the hands of the children of Ephraim, "Behold, this is the blessing of the everlasting God upon the tribes of Israel, and the richer blessing upon the head of Ephraim and his fellows" (D&C 133:30–34). This perfectly illustrates the concept of a chosen people. They are a people called, prepared, and chosen to be a light to others. They are deeply committed to the fulness of the gospel, which carries with it the responsibility to place the gospel crown upon all others who will receive it so that they too might then be lifted up and reign as kings and priests, queens and priestesses, throughout eternity (see Revelation 1:6; D&C 132:19–20).

The Knowledge of God

There is no salvation in ignorance, error, or superstition. In the great Intercessory Prayer, the Savior said that eternal life centered in knowing God and his Son, Jesus Christ (see John 17:3). Though the term is used with various shades of meaning, to *know* God in the purest scriptural sense is to have an intimate or covenant relationship with him. The Old Testament references to knowing God and to a man knowing his wife, meaning conceiving a child with her, both use the same Hebrew word, *yada*. As a man was to leave father and mother and cleave unto his wife and thus become one flesh with her, so he was to leave the things of the world, cleave unto his God, and become one with him. As faithfulness in marriage was essential to the nurturing of love, so faithfulness in keeping gospel covenants was understood to be necessary in obtaining a knowledge of God. As love of spouse was strengthened in sacrifice and devotion, so the knowledge of God was obtained in living those covenants with exactness and honor. Thus a frequent characteristic of Hebrew prophecy was to describe apostasy through the metaphor of adultery, and Israel's covenant with God as a marriage (see Jeremiah 2:20–37; Ezekiel 16; Hosea 1–3).

Similarly, we read in the New Testament that Joseph did not know Mary until after the birth of Christ (see Matthew 1:25) and that life eternal is to know God and Jesus Christ his son (see John 17:3). Both passages use the same Greek word, *ginosko*. One dictionary defines knowledge thus:

> Knowledge was not reducible to an act of the intellect that apprehended an object. The world preserves an experiential dimension that is characteristic of it: to observe, to experience, to know, to discern, to appraise, to establish an intimate relationship between two persons, whence to choose, to elect, to enter a sexual union, finally, to recognize. In conformity with this notion of truth, to know was to encounter someone; not to know was to thrust him aside from oneself. Knowledge of God was possible because this meant a "recognition" of the one who, through his creation, was already there. To know was to be disposed to obey. (Xavier Leon-Dufour, *Dictionary of the New Testament*, p. 259.)

Salvation Centers in Making Covenants

Only a God who is a personal being can be a covenant-making God. If God's perfection is found in the form of an abstract spirit, then a bodily resurrection is not a necessary reality. Abstract spirits do not give birth to children in their image and likeness, nor do they speak to them and make covenants with them. The God of the prophets and of the scriptures was always a covenant-making God and thus a personal being. Such is the God of whom we bear record. He is literally the Father of our spirits. He knows us as his children. We are his heirs and are in his image and likeness, both physically and spiritually. We have the ability and capacity to become as he is. As a loving parent he speaks to us and makes covenants with us.

It was in our first estate that we were first taught the saving principles of the gospel. Gospel principles no more originate in this life than we do. We learned them first in heaven. They are godly principles, and they are thus the principles by which our Eternal Father sought to raise his children. This explains why they have such a strong ring of familiarity when taught to us in this life. We know and recognize the truths of salvation as we do an old friend. Missionary work is not a matter of conversion—meaning that those being taught must always reverse their course or exchange old views for new ones—but instead a matter of remembering or awakening to truths once known and lived. Embracing the gospel is part of the process of returning home. There is a nostalgic spirit about it. It centers in family and friends. It centers in a mutually shared responsibility. The gospel covenant rings true in our soul's memory because we know of it already. That is what it means, in one sense, to be born in the covenant.

One of the distinctive characteristics of true religion is that it is family centered. Families in turn are the creation of sacred covenants between a man, a woman, and God. The notion that salvation is to be found independent of the family unit is, to borrow a phrase from Joseph Smith, "an old sectarian notion, and is false." The Apostle Paul said that we work out our salvation with fear and trembling (see Philippians 2:12–13), but what we don't do is work it out independent of Christ or of each other. Our covenant is to help and strengthen one another. Heaven is a great family reunion, not a hermitage. If it were intended to be a solitary place, then it would follow that the way to work out our salvation would be to flee into the desert or the mountains to live alone, to avoid association with one another. But God said that it was not good for man to be alone, and he created a help meet for him (see Genesis 2:18).

Perhaps Eden's most sacred moment was when God united Adam and Eve as husband and wife. With that union came the charge to multiply and replenish the earth. Why? Because salvation is a family affair. Families are the order of heaven, and they derive from covenants. What God did not say to the newly married couple was, "Now live alone in solitude, look after yourselves, and get saved." Why? Because there is no salvation in such a course. Heaven is not a convent, not a place of everlasting solitude, but rather a place where the joys of creation and birth are as endless and expansive as love itself.

Elder Boyd K. Packer related an experience that highlights the importance of becoming a covenant people.

> Several years ago I installed a stake president in England. . . . He had an unusual sense of direction. He was like a mariner with a sextant who took his bearings from the stars. I met with him each time he came to conference and was impressed that he kept himself and his stake on course.
>
> Fortunately for me, when it was time for his release, I was assigned to reorganize the stake. It was then that I discovered what that sextant was and how he adjusted it to check his position and get a bearing for himself and for his members.
>
> He accepted his release, and said: "I was happy to accept the call to serve as stake president, and I am equally happy to accept my release. I did not serve just because I was under *call*. I served because I am under *covenant*. And I can keep my covenants quite as well as a home teacher as I can serving as stake president."
>
> This president understood the word *covenant*.
>
> While he was neither a scriptorian nor a gospel scholar, he somehow had learned that exaltation is achieved by keeping covenants, not by holding high position.
>
> The mariner gets his bearing from light coming from celestial bodies—the sun by day, the stars by night. That stake president did not need a mariner's sextant to set his course. In his mind there was a sextant infinitely more refined and precise than any mariner's instrument.

Elder Packer concluded the analogy: "The spiritual sextant, which each of us has, also functions on the principle of light from celestial sources. Set that sextant in your mind to the word *covenant* or the word *ordinance*. The light will come through. Then you can fix your position and set a true course in life." (Conference Report, April 1987, pp. 26–27.)

Elder Parley P. Pratt declared:

> If I were a Jew, you might cry to me and preach to me until doomsday, and then take a sword, and hold it over me to sever my head from my body, but I should say, I will not move one step to the standard that *is* not Abraham's, nor from the everlasting covenant in which my fathers Abraham, Isaac, and Jacob, and all the holy Prophets will come and sit down in the presence of God, upon the same principles with their modern children. I am a Jew, and my hope is in the covenants of the fathers. If you nations who are not numbered in that covenant wish to be blessed, it must be in that covenant, and in no other way; and you cannot bring me any other standard that is a lawful one. You may teach me Christianity, as you call it; you may try to govern me by a republican government, as you call it; and ten thousand other things; but when you have taught them all to me, neither for your fire, your sword, your government, your religion, your threats, nor anything else will I ever embrace any other system but the standard, the covenant, in which all my nation, all the Ten Tribes and the scattered remnants can be blessed; a covenant that will look them up, with all the Gentile world; and raise all the ancients from the dead, and by which all can sit down together in the same kingdom, and be governed by the same principles, covenants, laws, and ordinances for ever. (*JD* 1:180–81.)

Such, Elder Pratt would reason, should be the position of all Bible believers. They ought not be one whit behind the Jews in adherence to that same standard or in their allegiance to the promise of blessings via the covenant God made with Abraham. God has not ceased to be God, and his covenants and promises have not ceased to be eternal.

Conclusion

In a revelation given to the Prophet Joseph Smith, the Lord returned again to the metaphor of salt to remind us of who we are.

"When men are called unto mine everlasting gospel, and covenant with an everlasting covenant," he said, "they are accounted as the salt of the earth and the savor of men; they are called to be the savor of men; therefore, if that salt of the earth lose its savor, behold, it is thenceforth good for nothing only to be cast out and trodden under the feet of men" (D&C 101:39–40). A subsequent revelation adds: "For they were set to be a light unto the world, and to be the saviors of men; and inasmuch as they are not the saviors of men, they are as salt that has lost its savor, and is thenceforth good for nothing but to be cast out and trodden under foot of men" (D&C 103:9–10).

By covenant—a covenant made long before our birth into mortality—we agreed to be the salt of the earth, the conduit for the knowledge and power of salvation unto all people. As salt is used in almost limitless ways, we as a chosen people are destined to serve, lead, lift, inspire, and bless others in countless ways. Ours are to be lives of service; such was our covenant, and such is our destiny. To that end we have been given the following charge: "Search diligently, pray always, and be believing, and all things shall work together for your good, if ye walk uprightly and remember the covenant wherewith ye have covenanted one with another" (D&C 90:24).

4

The History of Histories

> *I am the Lord your God, even the God of your fathers, the God of Abraham and of Isaac and of Jacob. I am he who led the children of Israel out of the land of Egypt; and my arm is stretched out in the last days, to save my people Israel.*
> —D&C 136:21–22

From latter-day revelation we learn that the Lord's government is patriarchal. The family is the fundamental unit of that government. All mankind are the spirit children of God, with whom we lived, perhaps for countless ages, before our birth into mortality. When men were first placed on earth, the only government known to them was patterned after that which they had known in the heavens. It was a perfect theocratic, patriarchal system with father Adam at the head. This system prevailed among the righteous from Adam to the time of Abraham and beyond. This system, which governed both the temporal and the spiritual affairs, is known as the patriarchal order.

From Adam to Abraham

When the office of patriarch was restored in this dispensation, a revelation followed that explained that this "order of the priesthood was confirmed to be handed down from father to son, and rightly belongs to the literal descendants of the chosen seed, to whom the promises were made." The revelation then notes that "this order was instituted in the days of Adam" and was handed down by the laying on of hands from Adam to Seth. In ordaining Seth, Adam promised him "that his posterity should be the chosen of the Lord, and that they should be preserved unto the end of the earth." Others also received this order of the priesthood under the hand of Adam. (D&C 107:40–50.)

Enoch, the seventh from Adam, was also ordained under Adam's hand (see D&C 107:48). In a great panoramic vision of the earth's future, Enoch witnessed the Flood at the time of Noah. Attendant to that experience, the Lord covenanted with him that a remnant of his seed would always be found among the nations of the earth (see Moses 7:51–52). For that reason, Methuselah, his son, was not translated with others of the righteous who were caught up into heaven. Methuselah, in turn, "prophesied that from his loins should spring all the kingdoms of the earth (through Noah), and he took glory unto himself" (Moses 8:3).

The covenant that the Lord made with Enoch was made anew with Noah. To him the Lord said: "I will establish my covenant with you, which I made unto Enoch, concerning the remnants of your posterity. And God made a covenant with Noah, and said, This shall be the token of the covenant I make between me and you, and for every living creature with you, for perpetual generations; I will set my bow in the cloud; and it shall be for a token of a covenant between me and the earth." That covenant included the promise that the earth would not again be destroyed by flood. Further, the Lord explained that he would remember his covenant with Enoch and that when men sought to keep all of his commandments, the city of Enoch would return to the earth. "And this is mine everlasting covenant," the Lord said, "that when thy posterity shall embrace the truth, and look upward, then shall Zion look downward, and all the heavens shall shake with gladness, and the earth shall tremble with joy; and the general assembly of the church of the first-born shall come down out of heaven, and possess the earth, and shall have place until the end come. And this is mine everlasting covenant, which I made with thy father Enoch." (JST Genesis 9:17–23.)

Later these promises were to become the inheritance of Noah's son Shem (see JST Genesis 9:30). Shem, in turn, became the father of the Semitic races and thus a progenitor of Abraham, who received this same patriarchal office from Melchizedek, who had "received it through the lineage of his fathers" reaching back to Noah, and through Noah back to Adam (see D&C 84:14–16). This doctrine of the priesthood, along with the attendant doctrines of a covenant and chosen people, were well known to Abraham long before the God of heaven made with him what we have come to know as the Abrahamic covenant. He recorded:

> I sought for the blessings of the fathers, and the right whereunto I should be ordained to administer the same; having been myself a follower of righteousness, desiring also to be one who possessed great knowledge, and to be a greater follower of righteousness, and to possess a greater knowledge, and to be a father of many nations, a prince of peace, and desiring to receive instructions, and to keep the commandments of God, I became a rightful heir, a High Priest, holding the right belonging to the fathers.
>
> It was conferred upon me from the fathers; it came down from the fathers, from the beginning of time, yea, even from the beginning, or before the foundation of the earth, down to the present time, even the right of the firstborn, or the first man, who is Adam, or first father, through the fathers unto me.
>
> I sought for mine appointment unto the Priesthood according to the appointment of God unto the fathers concerning the seed. (Abraham 1:2–4.)

The Beginnings of Israel

Were the complete history of the house of Israel to be written, "it would be the history of histories, the key of the world's history for the past twenty centuries" (Little and Richards, *A Compendium of the Doctrines of the Gospel*, p. 85). Israel's history begins with the Lord's command to Abram to leave Ur of the Chaldees and go to a land that would be shown him. From the beginning, his was to be a journey of faith. He was to leave both his father's house and his kindred, trusting entirely in the Lord for direction. With Abram went Sarai, his wife; Lot, his brother's son; and Lot's wife. Later his father, Terah, would follow them. They journeyed to a land that they named Haran, after Abram's brother who had died in the famine that gripped the land of Ur. It was there that the Lord appeared to Abram, telling him to take

Lot and continue his journey to the land of Canaan (see Abraham 2:1–6).

When Abram and Sarai again resumed their journey, they took with them the "souls that [they] had won in Haran" (Abraham 2:15; Genesis 12:5). The size of their company is not hinted at, but not long afterward, when Abram was called on to give chase to Lot's captors, he took with him three hundred and eighteen fighting men. Remember, this is after he and Lot had parted company, so it is not unreasonable to suppose that a goodly number of souls companied with Lot. If these fighting men and their families were those converted in Haran, it would justify the Talmudic tradition that the name *Abraham* (which means "father of multitudes or nations") "is really the father of proselytes" (Ginzberg, *Legends of the Jews* 5:233). Abraham, it is said, made his proselytes among the men while Sarai converted the women (see Ginzberg, 1:203).

The Abrahamic Covenant

According to the chronology of the book of Abraham, it was at this time that the Lord made with Abram what we have come to know as the Abrahamic covenant. Because of this and other revelations of the Restoration, our understanding of the importance of this event goes well beyond that of the rest of the Bible-believing world. This understanding, which embraces the knowledge that Abram and Sarai entered into what we know as the new and everlasting covenant of marriage, stands as a classic illustration of the plain and precious things taken from the Old Testament text. As a reminder of this covenant, the Lord changed Abram's name to Abraham and Sarai's name to Sarah. The name *Abram* means "exalted father," while his new name meant "father of nations" or "father of multitudes." The name *Sarah* means "princess." Thus, their new names typified the Lord's promise of endless kingdoms and endless posterity.

The book of Genesis preserves the promise that from Abraham would come a great nation, that his name would be great, and that in him all families of the earth would be blessed. He was also promised that those who blessed him would be blessed and that those who cursed him would be cursed (see Genesis 12:2–3). The Old Testament also contains the promise that the land of Canaan would be granted to

Abraham's posterity as an everlasting possession (see Genesis 17:6–8). Further, Abraham was promised that his seed would be as numerous as the stars of the heaven or the sand upon the seashore and that through his seed all the nations of the earth would be blessed (see Genesis 22:17–18).

It is, however, in the book of Abraham that we learn that these blessings were the result of a covenant that Abraham made with the Lord. From this text we learn that the special promise to his seed is that they will receive the gospel, hold the priesthood, and take its blessings to all the nations and kindreds of the earth. It is Abraham's seed who have been commissioned to carry the gospel message and its saving covenants to all the children of men. "I will bless them that bless thee," the Lord promised, "and curse them that curse thee; and in thee (that is, in thy Priesthood) and in thy seed (that is, thy Priesthood), for I give unto thee a promise that this right shall continue in thee, and in thy seed after thee (that is to say, the literal seed, or the seed of the body) shall all the families of the earth be blessed, even with the blessings of the Gospel, which are the blessings of salvation, even of life eternal" (Abraham 2:11). Referring to this covenant, Christ reminded the Nephites that they were the seed of Abraham and that their posterity would be among those who took the blessings of the Holy Ghost to all the families of the earth (see 3 Nephi 20:27).

Obviously, before Abraham received this covenant he had been baptized and had the priesthood conferred upon him. This covenant embraces the promise that his marriage with Sarah was to be eternal. The knowledge that this covenant is completely centered in the gospel—growing out of baptism and the priesthood—and in the promise of eternal marriage and the continuation of the family unit has been taken from the Old Testament. That this was clearly understood even into New Testament times is illustrated in Paul's epistle to the Galatians, in which he makes reference to Abraham's sharing the gospel of Jesus Christ. It was that same gospel, Paul taught, that was to bless all the nations of the earth (see Galatians 3:8; see also *Teachings*, pp. 59–60).

Part of the dialogue between God and Abraham in announcing this covenant has been restored to us in the Joseph Smith Translation:

> And God talked with him, saying, My people have gone astray from my precepts, and have not kept mine ordinances, which I gave unto their fathers;

> And they have not observed mine anointing, and the burial, or baptism wherewith I commanded them;
>
> But have turned from the commandment, and taken unto themselves the washing of children, and the blood of sprinkling;
>
> And have said that the blood of the righteous Abel was shed for sins; and have not known wherein they are accountable before me (JST Genesis 17:4–7).

This description of the apostasy in Abraham's day also indicates that Abraham knew the gospel ordinances, including baptism by immersion, before the time of what we call the Abrahamic covenant. These principles had come down through the fathers from the time of Adam (see D&C 107:40–42).

The Covenant Lineage

The Bible is in large measure the history of Abraham's family and the foreshadowing of how the Lord's promises to him are to be fulfilled. The Lord commanded Abraham to leave Ur of Chaldees because its inhabitants were undesirable for intermarriage with his family. As a descendant of Shem, Abraham held the right by birth to bear the priesthood. For three generations this family intermarried in order that the bloodline might be kept pure. Abraham and his brother Nahor married their brother Haran's daughters. Nahor's son Bethuel became the father of Rebekah. Rebekah became the wife of Abraham's son Isaac. Laban, also the son of Nahor, became the father of Leah and Rachel, the wives of Jacob, Isaac and Rebekah's son.

Jacob also married Bilhah and Zilpah, the maids of Leah and Rachel. According to the apocryphal Testament of Naphtali, these two women were also of the same race as Abraham and Shem (see Naphtali 1:9–12). Through Jacob, whose name was changed to Israel, the promised blessings were extended to his twelve sons. In each instance, those portions of the Abrahamic covenant that pertain to personal exaltation and eternal increase were renewed with the generations of Abraham as they entered into the same covenants with God that their illustrious father had done before them. The covenant was renewed in full with Isaac (see Genesis 24:60; 26:1–4, 24) and again with Jacob (see Genesis 28:13–14; 35:9–13; 48:3–4).

Since Reuben, Jacob's oldest son, forfeited his birthright through immorality, it was passed to Rachel's first son, Joseph (see 1 Chronicles 5:1–2). Joseph's two sons were adopted by Jacob and blessed by him. Thus Joseph received a double portion of his father's blessings as part of his birthright. While in Egypt, Joseph took as wife Asenath, the daughter of the priest of On. Many have supposed she was an Egyptian and thus not of the Semitic race. While the scriptures are silent about her genealogy, the available historical evidence indicates that Asenath was probably a Shemite princess born in Egypt. Scholars are generally agreed that Joseph was in Egypt during what has become known as the dynasties of the Hyksos or shepherd kings. While the origins of these people are uncertain, it appears that by about 1700 B.C. or a little earlier, they had installed themselves at first in the region of the Nile Delta, later being able to control the whole, or at least much of Egypt. It is believed that in composition they were largely Semitic. From Joseph the birthright passed to Ephraim, and through Ephraim to his tribe even to this day (see Jeremiah 31:6–9).

When Jacob and the seventy members of his family moved to Egypt, they were favored by Pharaoh, one of the shepherd kings, with the land of Goshen. There the children of Israel "increased abundantly, and multiplied, and waxed exceeding mighty; and the land was filled with them." Then a king arose who "knew not Joseph." He feared that the tribes of Israel, who had remained a separate people, might unite with Egypt's enemies and fight against her. Thus taskmasters were set over Israel to afflict and burden them. "But the more they afflicted them, the more they multiplied and grew." (Exodus 1:7–14.) Thus bondage became their bitter lot. Nevertheless, the Lord had given Joseph the promise that he would "raise up Moses," who would gather Israel and "lead them as a flock" (JST Genesis 50:34). So it was that Moses united Israel as a nation and led them out of Egyptian bondage. Their army of over 600,000 men suggests that the population of the united nation must have numbered in the millions.

To dramatize the absolute necessity of Israel being true to her covenants and remaining a separate people, God commanded them to "utterly destroy" the seven nations that then inhabited their promised land of Canaan. They were not to make covenant with them or show any mercy to them, neither were they to enter into any marriages with them, for should they do so they too were to be destroyed. (See Deuteronomy 7:14.) Moses also directed that when they crossed the

Jordan and entered the promised land, memorial stones were to be set up and sacrifices were to be offered on Mount Ebal. The ceremony prescribed by Moses required six of the tribes—Simeon, Levi, Judah, Issachar, Joseph, and Benjamin, those who sprang from the freeborn wives of Jacob—to stand on Mount Gerizim, while the other tribes, the descendants of Leah's and Rachel's maids—Gad, Asher, Zebulun, Dan, and Naphtali, with Reuben (who on account of Reuben's sin was added to their number)—were to stand on Mount Ebal. Then the priests in the vale between the two mounts were to turn toward Gerizim and read to those upon Mount Gerizim the blessings promised in the law. The people responded with an "Amen!" Then the priests turned toward Ebal and read the cursings that would be Israel's should she not be true to her covenants, and again the people gave their solemn assent. In this dramatic fashion the tribes of Israel covenanted to be blessed in obedience and cursed in disobedience. An altar was then built upon Ebal and plastered with lime, upon which was written "all the words of this law very plainly." (Deuteronomy 27:4–13; Joshua 8:30–35.)

Among the curses to come upon Israel should she be untrue to her covenants was the scattering "among all people, from the one end of the earth even unto the other." It was prophesied that in this dispersal she would serve false gods, know no ease, suffer "sorrow of mind," and have her very life "hang in doubt" both day and night. So great would be her suffering that "in the morning" she would say, "Would God it were even!" and when the evening finally arrived she would be found saying, "Would God it were morning!" (Deuteronomy 28:64–67.)

The Dispersion of Israel

Israel held together as a family for over 300 years of rule by the judges and another 120 years under the kings—Saul, David, and Solomon. Indeed, so glorious was David's reign, which included gaining possession of Jerusalem, that it is looked upon as the pattern for God's future kingdom on earth. Yet such glory was short lived, for under the wicked rule of Solomon's son, Rehoboam, the kingdom was divided; in approximately 975 B.C. Judah and much of Benjamin chose to stand with Rehoboam. The rest of Israel, usually identified as the ten tribes—or as Israel or Ephraim, its most prominent tribe—were led by Jeroboam, an Ephraimite. For about 250 years the two kingdoms maintained a separate existence. In 721 B.C., the ten tribes were taken captive by the Assyrians under Shalmanezer and Sargon and led off into Assyria—whence they are believed later to have left for an undetermined land. About a century after the fall of the northern kingdom the southern kingdom was brought to an end by the Babylonians under Nebuchadnezzar. As Jeremiah had prophesied, they remained in captivity for seventy years (see Jeremiah 25:11–12), until the Persians under Cyrus captured Babylon and granted the Jews the privilege of returning to Judea and rebuilding their temple, according to Isaiah's prophecy (see Isaiah 44:28; 45:1–25).

Though multitudes of the exiles returned, many did not, instead scattering themselves among various lands. Those that returned were unable to regain their former power and were never again a truly independent people. They were assailed in turn by Syria, Egypt, and Rome, to whom they were in bondage during Christ's ministry. Rejecting the Messiah, the nation of the Jews brought upon themselves the curses against which they had been warned. The army of Rome destroyed Jerusalem and its temple in A.D. 70, leaving not one stone standing upon another. A once-proud nation was then scattered among all the nations of the earth.

After those of the northern kingdom had been led captive by Assyria, they disappeared so completely that they have since become known as the lost tribes. Nephi, speaking some six hundred years before the ministry of Christ, said, "The more part of all the tribes have been led away; and they are scattered to and fro upon the isles of the sea; and whither they are none of us knoweth, save that we know that they have been led away" (1 Nephi 22:4). When the Savior visited the Nephites, he indicated that the Father had commanded him to visit "other sheep" whom we presume were those of the lost tribes (see 3 Nephi 16:1–4). Following the Savior's visit, the lost tribes, like their Nephite counterparts, fell into apostasy (see Jacob 5:39). In their apostate condition, they too lost the knowledge of their identity as a covenant people and, in fulfillment of the ancient prophecies, were also scattered to the ends of the earth.

The Leaven of the Earth

In the economy of God, whose works cannot be frustrated, scattered Israel is to be a leaven of righteousness among all nations. When the books are opened and the history of mankind is made known, it will be with great surprise that even the Judeo-Christian world will discover the literalness of Bible prophecy. The seed of Abraham will always be found on the frontier of movements that bring freedom and prepare the way for righteousness. Such is the blood that has led in breaking the "shackles of kingcraft and priestcraft and oppression of every kind" (Erastus Snow, *JD* 23:186).

It has been Ephraim's children who have stood as sentinels down through the centuries, "soldiers of God" (for that is the meaning of *Israel*) who have tirelessly and fearlessly fought so that truth and freedom might come to all. Such was the blood of the many martyrs whose sacrifice was necessary to bring forth the Bible. The Prophet Joseph Smith is reported to have said after reading a book about Christian martyrs, "I have, by the aid of the Urim and Thummin, seen those martyrs and they were honest, devoted followers of Christ according to the light they possessed, [and] they will be saved" (*Reminiscences of Joseph, the Prophet, and the Coming Forth of the Book of Mormon*, pp. 5–6). Such was the nobility of those great souls raised up by the hand of God to lay the foundations of a government under whose protection the restoration of the gospel could take place, and under the protection of whose flag messengers might go to all the nations of the earth to search out the scattered remnant of Jacob.

It was for this purpose that God raised up George Washington, Thomas Jefferson, Benjamin Franklin, John Adams, and other patriots, all inspired men—though some of them knew it not—"who carved out with their swords and with their pens the character and stability of this great government which they hoped would stand forever, an asylum for the oppressed of all nations, where no man's religion would be questioned, no man would be limited in his honest service to his Maker, so long as he did not infringe upon the rights of his fellow men" (Orson F. Whitney, *JD* 26:200). It was upon their determination, courage, and loyalty to God that the republic of the United States was established. It was these men, prodded by the hand of the Almighty, who provided the resting place, as it were, "for the Ark of the covenant, where the temple of our God might be built," where the gospel could be restored, and practiced in freedom, where not so much as "a dog would wag his tongue in opposition to the purposes of the Almighty" (Ibid., p. 201). Many of these very souls appeared to Wilford Woodruff in the St. George Temple, requesting that the saving ordinances of the gospel be performed for them. " 'We laid the foundation of the government you now enjoy,' " they declared, " 'and we never apostatized from it, but we remained true to it and were faithful to God.' " These, Elder Woodruff testified, were the signers of the Declaration of Independence. (JD 19:229.)

Conclusion

Not only has the world forgotten the God of the ancients, but her spiritual amnesia has also included God's covenant with Abraham and his seed, even blotting from her mind God's right to call his own prophets and priests. With a total disregard for the promises and restrictions of old, the world has freely concocted its priesthoods and gospels. Yet if ours is to be the God of Abraham, Isaac, and Jacob, then ours must be the faith of the ancient fathers also, and if ours be the ancient faith, it must be a faith that centers in the promises made to the fathers—promises that extend to their righteous progeny, even to the end of time.

5

The Morning Breaks, the Shadows Flee

> *Jehovah speaks! Let earth give ear, and Gentile nations*
> *turn and live. His mighty arm is making bare,*
> *his covenant people to receive.*
> —Parley P. Pratt

The entire story of the Restoration, as it centers in the opening of the heavens to Joseph Smith, is but the fulfilling of God's promises to Abraham. Israel's history anciently is but the foreshadowing of Israel's history in the last days. If God spoke anciently, he must speak today. If he remembered his promises to a beleaguered Israel, if he called prophets, restored the priesthood, gathered the people, performed miracles, and led them to a land of promise anciently, so he must today. As a child is in the image of his parents, so the events of the last days are patterned after those of former days. Ours is the story of restoration, of a bringing back or a renewing of the glories of the past. Truly, as we sing with exultation, "The visions and blessings of old are returning" (*Hymns*, 1985, no. 2).

Restoring the Ancient Covenant

That none might miss the unfolding drama as promises made in ages past are fulfilled, the Lord told Joseph Smith that he was to hold the keys by which Israel was to "be led, and no more be confounded at all" (D&C 35:25). By revelation the Lord introduced himself to Joseph Smith as the "Mighty One of Israel" (D&C 36:1) and promised that "Israel shall be saved," stating, "I will lead them whithersoever I will, and no power shall stay my hand" (D&C 38:33). The Lord further instructed the Prophet: "Thou shalt preach the fulness of my gospel, which I have sent forth in these last days, the covenant which I have sent forth to recover my people, which are of the house of Israel" (D&C 39:11). Joseph the Seer was instructed that a New Jerusalem was to be built and Zion redeemed. "The redemption of Zion must needs come by power," the Lord said; "therefore, I will raise up unto my people a man, who shall lead them like as Moses led the children of Israel. For ye are the children of Israel, and of the seed of Abraham, and ye must needs be led out of bondage by power, and with a stretched-out arm. And as your fathers were led at the first, even so shall the redemption of Zion be." (D&C 103:15–18.) Is not this a story in the image of the past?

The Literal Seed of Abraham

That none might err, supposing this to be merely an analogy or figurative language and not literally the blood descendants of Israel gathering the blood descendants of Israel, the following revelation was given to Joseph Smith:

> Therefore, thus saith the Lord unto you, with whom the priesthood hath continued through the lineage of your fathers—
> For ye are lawful heirs, according to the flesh, and have been hid from the world with Christ in God—
> Therefore your life and the priesthood have remained, and must needs remain through you and your lineage until the restoration of all things spoken by the mouths of all the holy prophets since the world began.
> Therefore, blessed are ye if ye continue in my goodness, a light unto the Gentiles, and through this priesthood, a savior unto my people Israel. The Lord hath said it. Amen. (D&C 86:8–11.)

President Brigham Young testified:

It was decreed in the councils of eternity, long before the foundations of the earth were laid, that he [Joseph Smith] should be the man, in the last dispensation of this world, to bring forth the word of God to the people, and receive the fulness of the keys and power of the Priesthood of the Son of God. The Lord had his eyes upon him, and upon his father, and upon his father's father, and upon their progenitors clear back to Abraham, and from Abraham to the flood, from the flood to Enoch, and from Enoch to Adam. He has watched that family and that blood as it has circulated from its fountain to the birth of that man. He was foreordained in eternity to preside over this last dispensation. (JD 7:289-90.)

In like manner, Elder Heber C. Kimball testified that Joseph Smith "actually saw" in vision the early leaders of the Church and declared that they were all of one stock. "We were," he said, "positively heirs of the Priesthood; for he had seen us as such in his vision." Elder Kimball listed by name some that the Prophet had seen in vision, including himself, Brigham Young, Newel K. Whitney, and Oliver Cowdery. He indicated that there were twenty or thirty others that Joseph mentioned by name. (JD 5:215-16.)

Elder Parley P. Pratt wrote to one of his brothers, saying that Joseph had a vision and saw that the Pratts and the Smiths shared a common grandfather a few generations removed (see Bennett, *Saviors on Mount Zion*, p. 86). Speaking to the body of the Saints, Wilford Woodruff declared: "We are called of God. We have been gathered from the distant nations, and our lives have been hid with Christ in God, but we have not known it. The Lord has been watching over us from the hour of our birth. We are of the seed of Ephraim, and of Abraham, and of Joseph, who was sold into Egypt, and these are the instruments that God has kept in the spirit world to come forth in these latter days to take hold of this kingdom and build it up." (JD 22:233.)

Speaking of the leading brethren of Joseph's day, Brigham Young explained that they discovered they "all sprang back to the settlement of New England" some two hundred years before.

It is but a little more than that time when Father Smith, the Goddards, Richards, Youngs and Kimballs were all in one family—as it were. We are all relations. . . . You have heard Joseph say that the people did not know him; *he had his eyes on the relation to blood-relations. Some have supposed that he meant spirit, but it was the blood-relation. This is it that he referred to.* His descent from Joseph that was sold into Egypt was direct, and the blood was pure in him. That is why the Lord chose him; and we are pure when this blood-strain from Ephraim comes down pure. The decrees of the Almighty will be exalted—that blood which was in him was pure and he had the sole right and lawful power, as he was the legal heir to the blood that has been on the earth and has come down through a pure lineage. The union of various ancestors kept that blood pure. (*Utah Genealogical and Historical Magazine*, 1920, 11: 107–8, emphasis added.)

"These declarations of relationship between the Prophet's family and the Youngs and Kimballs and Richards were nothing short of prophetic," writes Archibald F. Bennett. "For in 1845 genealogical research was in its infancy, and only about thirty-six family genealogies had ever been printed in America. Heber C. Kimball had not been able to learn the names of even his grandparents, and Brigham Young knew no further than his great-grandparents. The Prophet knew back from himself five generations." (Bennett, *Saviors on Mount Zion*, p. 87.) Only recently has genealogical research been completed that verifies the claims of Joseph Smith and Brigham Young. It was long after their deaths that we learned that Joseph Smith, Oliver Cowdery, Wilford Woodruff, Parley and Orson Pratt, and Frederick G. Williams all descended from a Puritan preacher named John Lathrop. The Reverend John Lathrop had been imprisoned in England for teachings unacceptable to the Church of England, while his wife languished at home and died. He was later allowed to bring his family to America, where he became a noted preacher. Others now established as relatives of the Prophet include Heber C. Kimball, Lorenzo Snow, Willard Richards, and Franklin D. Richards. Predominant among the Prophet's forefathers were patriots, pioneers, and ministers. They ranked among the best men and women of their day. Many of his forefathers came to America seeking religious freedom; seven of them were on the Mayflower in 1620.

A Proclamation to All the World

There have been countless religious leaders and reformers, but one alone thought it necessary to establish his claim to authority by virtue of lineage. Thinking lineage important, he could have announced himself to be a descendant of the Romans or the Greeks. He could have claimed to be of the loins of Aristotle or Socrates or a descendant from some royal line, or he could have chosen descent from any number of kings. Yet Joseph Smith boldly claimed that he was of Abraham through Joseph of Egypt. Nor did he stop there, for he announced that the brethren who surrounded him in bearing witness to the message of the Restoration were of that same lineage, that together they would stand at the head of Ephraim, and that they would gather Israel from every nation, kindred, tongue, and people.

In 1845 the Quorum of the Twelve Apostles issued a proclamation to all the world in which they prophesied that

> as this work progresses in its onward course, and becomes more and more an object of political and religious interest and excitement, no king, ruler, or subject, no community or individual, will stand *neutral*. All will at length be influenced by one spirit or the other; and will take sides either for or against the kingdom of God, and the fulfilment of the prophets, in the great restoration and return of his long dispersed covenant people.
>
> Some will act the part of the venerable Jethro, the father-in-law of Moses; or the noble Cyrus; and will aid and bless the people of God; or like Ruth, the Moabitess, will forsake their people and their kindred and country, and will say to the Saints, or to Israel: "*This people shall be my people, and their God my God.*" While others will walk in the footsteps of a Pharaoh, or a Balak, and will harden their hearts, and fight against God, and seek to destroy his people. These will commune with priests and prophets who love the wages of unrighteousness; and who, like Balaam, will seek to curse, or to find enchantments against Israel. (*Messages of the First Presidency* 1:257.)

Thus out of "obscurity and out of darkness" has come the message of the Restoration, the establishment anew of the kingdom of God on the earth, which will now "roll forth unto the ends of the earth, as the stone which is cut out of the mountain without hands shall roll forth, until it has filled the whole earth" (D&C 65:2). The Lord's servants, most of them from the tribe of Ephraim, are now going forth to raise the "voice of warning" and "none shall stay them," for the Lord has "commanded them" (D&C 1:4–5). They will gather Israel, and in a yet future day all the tribes of Israel will "bring forth their rich treasures unto the children of Ephraim, my servants," the Lord said. "And the boundaries of the everlasting hills shall tremble at their presence. And there shall they fall down and be crowned with glory, even in Zion, by the hands of the servants of the Lord, even the children of Ephraim. And they shall be filled with songs of everlasting joy. Behold, this is the blessing of the everlasting God upon the tribes of Israel, and the richer blessing upon the head of Ephraim and his fellows." (D&C 133:30–34.)

The Ancient Order Restored

As Jesus spoke with his disciples at Caesarea Philippi, the chief Apostle, in response to a query by his Master, declared, "Thou art the Christ, the Son of the living God." Peter was commended for his witness and assured that such a testimony was of divine origin. "And I say also unto thee," the Savior continued, "That thou art Peter, and upon this rock I will build my church; and the gates of hell shall not prevail against it. And I will give unto thee the keys of the kingdom of heaven: and whatsoever thou shalt bind on earth shall be bound in heaven: and whatsoever thou shalt loose on earth shall be loosed in heaven." (Matthew 16:13–19.) Within a week the Lord's promise was fulfilled: Jesus took with him Peter, James, and John—the chief Apostles and First Presidency of the meridian Church—to a high mountain to pray. While in that setting, these four were transfigured—lifted spiritually to a higher plane—and thus prepared for a transcendent experience.

Moses and Elijah appeared and bestowed their keys upon this meridian Presidency. Keys are directing powers, the right of presidency. These rights and powers would allow the Apostles to govern and direct the Church in the absence of Jesus Christ and to make available to the members all of the blessings of the everlasting gospel. Peter, James, and John had received the Melchizedek Priesthood earlier and had been given apostolic power and commission at the time of their appointment to the Twelve. As a result of this experience on the Mount of Transfiguration they were granted the right to bind and seal on earth, with the full confidence that their actions would receive sealing validity in the heavens.

That which took place in the first-century Christian Church has its parallels in the latter-day Church. The winter and spring of 1836 proved to be an era of both modern Pentecost and modern transfiguration. By early April, bearers of the priesthood had been washed and anointed. On Sunday, 3 April 1836, one week following the glorious dedicatory service of the Kirtland Temple, the Saints were again assembled in the house of the Lord. In the morning hours Elder Thomas B. Marsh (then President of the Twelve) and Elder David W. Patten were called upon to speak. In the afternoon the First Presidency and the Apostles participated in a sacramental service, after which Joseph Smith and Oliver Cowdery knelt in prayer behind drawn curtains adjacent to the large pulpits on the west side of the main floor of the temple. At that moment a wondrous vision burst upon them, one of the most significant theophanies of the ages.

Just as Jesus and his three ancient Apostles were transfigured in the first century, so also were Joseph and Oliver—"apostles, and especial witnesses" of the name of Christ (D&C 27:12)—transformed and made ready to penetrate the veil and receive divine direction and authority. Appropriately, Jesus the Christ appeared first. In the wanderings of ancient Israel, Jehovah had chosen frequently to make his presence known and manifest his glory through a cloud that rested upon his temple. On this sacred day, Jehovah came again to his temple—the first to be authorized and accepted by him since the long night of apostate darkness. Our Lord's appearance was but the beginning of the realization of his promise given three years earlier: "And inasmuch as my people build a house unto me in the name of the Lord, and do not suffer any unclean thing to come into it, that it be not defiled, my glory shall rest upon it; yea, and my presence shall be there, for I will come into it, and all the pure in heart that shall come into it shall see God" (D&C 97:15–16). Jesus Christ accepted the offering of his Saints—this temple built at great sacrifice—and then expanded their vision in regard to the importance of that which they had accomplished: "Yea the hearts of thousands and tens of thousands shall greatly rejoice in consequence of the blessings which shall be poured out, and the endowment with which my servants have been endowed in this house" (D&C 110:9).

"After this vision [of the Savior] closed, the heavens were again opened unto us; and Moses appeared before us, and committed unto us the keys of the gathering of Israel from the four parts of the earth, and the leading of the ten tribes from the land of the north" (D&C 110:11). The keys or directing powers restored by the ancient lawgiver formalized the work of gathering that had begun earlier. They enabled the Saints to accomplish the directive delivered in September 1830: "And ye are called to bring to pass the gathering of mine elect; for mine elect hear my voice and harden not their hearts" (D&C 29:7). To the President of The Church of Jesus Christ of Latter-day Saints—the man appointed "to preside over the whole church, and to be like unto Moses" (D&C 107:91)—were given keys to gather modern Israel. Even as Moses led ancient Israel out of Egyptian bondage, so the President of the Church was given keys to lead modern Israel out of the bondage and throes of modern Egypt into Zion. As we shall discuss in detail in the next chapter, people are gathered first spiritually and then temporally. They are gathered first as they accept the true Messiah and are "restored to the true church and fold of God" (2 Nephi 9:2); they are gathered second as they congregate to the places where the Saints of God are. Only through the eventual establishment of stakes throughout the world can the full concept of Zion be realized; only then will the full blessings of the temple be had by all peoples.

"After this, Elias appeared, and committed the dispensation of the gospel of Abraham, saying that in us and our seed all generations after us should be blessed" (D&C 110:12). The identity of Elias—whether he be Noah, Melchizedek, Abraham himself, or a prophet named Elias from the days of Abraham—is not clearly known. In any case, this heavenly messenger restored the keys necessary to establish the ancient patriarchal order, making Joseph Smith and the faithful Saints who receive celestial marriage heirs to the blessings and "promises made to the fathers"—Abraham, Isaac, and Jacob. Elias thus restored the power by which eternal families are organized through the new and everlasting covenant of marriage. "As the crowning cause for wonderment," Elder Bruce R. McConkie has explained, "that God who is no respecter of persons has given a like promise [to that of Abraham and Joseph Smith] to every [member] in the kingdom who has gone to the holy temple and entered into the blessed order of matrimony there performed. Every person married in the temple for time and for all eternity has sealed upon him, conditioned upon his faithfulness, all of the blessings of the ancient patriarchs, including the crowning promise and assurance of eternal increase, which means, literally, a posterity as numerous as the dust particles of the earth." (*The Millennial Messiah*, p. 264.)

"After this vision had closed, another great and glorious vision burst upon us; for Elijah the prophet, who was taken to heaven without tasting death, stood before us, and said: Behold, the time has fully come, which was spoken of by the mouth of Malachi—testifying that he [Elijah] should be sent, before the great and dreadful day of the Lord come—to turn the hearts of the fathers to the children, and the children to the fathers, lest the whole earth be smitten with a curse" (D&C 110:13–15). Precisely on the day that Elijah's appearance took place, Jews throughout the world were engaged in the celebration of the Passover. Since the time of Malachi—from about 450–400 B.C. until now—Jews worldwide have awaited Elijah's coming with anxious anticipation. Elijah did come, but not to Jewish homes; he came rather to a synagogue of the Saints and to his legal administrators on earth. There he bestowed keys of inestimable worth.

When Moroni appeared to Joseph Smith in 1823 he quoted numerous passages from the Old and New Testaments. The Prophet indicated in his official history that Moroni quoted Malachi 4:5–6 but gave a different rendering from that in the King James Version. Malachi (through whom this promise came), we learn from the Prophet, "had his eye fixed on the restoration of the priesthood" (D&C 128:17). The prophecy began: "Behold, I will reveal unto you the Priesthood, by the hand of Elijah the prophet, before the coming of the great and dreadful day of the Lord" (Joseph Smith—History 1:38; D&C 2:1). Joseph and Oliver had been ordained to the Melchizedek Priesthood and been given apostolic power and commission as early as 1829. How was it, then, that Elijah would reveal the priesthood? Simply stated, Elijah was sent in 1836 to reveal keys of the priesthood and sealing powers that had not yet been fully understood or were not fully operational in this dispensation. Elijah restored the keys whereby families (organized in the patriarchal order through the powers delivered by Elias) could be bound and sealed for eternity.

Three months before his death, Joseph Smith instructed the Latter-day Saints concerning the mission of Elijah: "The spirit, power, and calling of Elijah is, that ye have power to hold the key of the revelations, ordinances, oracles, powers and endowments of the fulness of the Melchizedek Priesthood and of the kingdom of God on the earth" (*Teachings*, p. 337). Elijah restored the keys whereby individuals and families may (through the blessings of the holy temple) develop line upon line to the point where they receive the fulness of the priesthood and thus become kings and queens, priests and priestesses unto God in the patriarchal order. "Those holding the fulness of the Melchizedek Priesthood," Joseph had taught earlier, "are kings and priests of the Most High God, holding the keys of power and blessings" (*Teachings*, p. 322). Through the powers delivered by Elias—the new and everlasting covenant of marriage, the order entered into by Abraham, Isaac, and Jacob—eternal families are created, here and hereafter. Through the powers delivered by Elijah, man and wife may be sealed unto eternal life, inasmuch as "the power of Elijah is sufficient to make our calling and election sure" (*Teachings*, p. 338).

Elijah came to "plant in the hearts of the children the promises made to the fathers" whereby the "hearts of the children [should] turn to their fathers" (Joseph Smith—History 1:39; D&C 2:2). The Spirit of the Lord witnesses to faithful Latter-day Saints of the central place of eternal marriage and of the sublime joys associated with the everlasting continuation of the family. Through temples, God's promises to the fathers—the promises pertaining to the gospel, the priesthood, and eternal increase (see Abraham 2:8–11)—are extended to all the faithful Saints of all ages. The hearts of the children turn to the ancient fathers because the children are now participants in and recipients of the blessings of the fathers. Being profoundly grateful for such privileges, members of the Church (motivated by the *spirit* of Elijah) also find their hearts turning to their more immediate fathers, and do all within their power (through family history research and attendant temple work) to ensure that the blessings of Abraham, Isaac, and Jacob are enjoyed by ancestry as well as posterity. "If it were not so [that is, if Elijah had not come], the whole earth would be utterly wasted at [Christ's] coming" (Joseph Smith—History 1:39; D&C 2:3). Why? Because the earth would not have accomplished its foreordained purpose—to establish on its face a family system patterned after the order of heaven. If there were no sealing powers whereby families could be bound together, then the earth would never "answer the end of its creation" (D&C 49:16). It would be wasted and cursed, for all men and women would be forever without root or branch, without ancestry or posterity. However, because Elijah came, all other ordinances for the living and the dead (baptisms, confirmations, ordinations, sealings, etc.) have real meaning and are of efficacy, virtue, and force in eternity (see *Teachings*, p. 172; see also Joseph Fielding Smith, *Doctrines of Salvation* 2:115–28).

In summary, Moses restored the keys to gather Israel, to bring people into the Church and kingdom through missionary work. Elias restored the keys to organize those converts into eternal families through the covenant and ordinance of eternal marriage. And Elijah restored the keys associated with the fulness of the priesthood, the powers necessary to bind and seal those families unto eternal life. The ordinances associated with the ministry and bestowal of keys by Moses, Elias, and Elijah (culminating in temples of the Lord) are the capstone blessings of the gospel and the consummation of the Father's work: they provide purpose and perspective for all other gospel principles and ordinances.

Joseph Smith, a Modern Abraham

In September 1823 the angel Moroni appeared to the Prophet Joseph Smith. "This messenger proclaimed himself," Joseph wrote to John Wentworth, "to be an angel of God, sent to bring the joyful tidings that the covenant which God made with ancient Israel was at hand to be fulfilled, that the preparatory work for the second coming of the Messiah was speedily to commence; that the time was at hand for the Gospel in all its fullness to be preached in power, unto all nations that a people might be prepared for the Millennial reign. I was informed that I was chosen to be an instrument in the hands of God to bring about some of His purposes in this glorious dispensation." (*History of the Church* 4:536–37.) Joseph of old prophesied that his latter-day namesake would be a "choice seer," one who would be raised up by God to bring the people of the last days to the knowledge of the covenants that God had made with the ancient fathers (see 2 Nephi 3:7; compare 1 Nephi 13:26). The name *Joseph* is a significant name. Whether the name is taken from the Hebrew word

Yasaf, which means "to add," or from the word *Asaf*, meaning "to gather," one senses that the latter-day seer was destined to perform a monumental labor in regard to the fulfillment of the Abrahamic covenant in this final dispensation.

Joseph Smith becomes a "father of the faithful" to those of this dispensation, the means by which the chosen lineage is identified, gathered, organized as families, and sealed forevermore into the house of Israel to their God. Joseph Smith, Sr., the first patriarch, thus blessed his son as follows: "A marvelous work and a wonder has the Lord wrought by thy hand, even that which shall prepare the way for the remnants of his people to come in among the Gentiles, with their fulness, as the tribes of Israel are restored. I bless thee with the blessings of thy Fathers Abraham, Isaac and Jacob; and even the blessings of thy father Joseph, the son of Jacob. Behold, he looked after his posterity in the last days, when they should be scattered and driven by the Gentiles." (*Utah Genealogical and Historical Magazine*, vol. 23, October 1932, p. 175, as cited in Joseph F. McConkie, *His Name Shall Be Joseph*, p. 103.)

Through Joseph Smith the blessings of Abraham, Isaac, and Jacob are available to all who will join the Church and prove worthy of the blessings of the temple. Jehovah's plea through Isaiah that the people of the covenant become a light to the nations so that they might be his "salvation unto the end of the earth" (Isaiah 49:6) is thus realized through the restoration of the gospel. Thereby, as Joseph Smith himself declared, "the election of the promised seed still continues, and in the last day, they shall have the Priesthood restored unto them, and they shall be the 'saviors on Mount Zion' " (*Teachings*, p. 189). Because Joseph Smith was the head of this dispensation and its modern Abraham, Brigham Young could appropriately say of his predecessor: "Joseph is a father to Ephraim and to all Israel in these last days" (Journal History, 9 April 1837).

The Lord has repeatedly affirmed the special status of the latter-day prophet-leader: "As I said unto Abraham concerning the kindreds of the earth, even so I say unto my servant Joseph: In thee and in thy seed shall the kindred of the earth be blessed" (D&C 124:58). Further: "Abraham received promises concerning his seed, and of the fruit of his loins—from whose loins ye are, namely, my servant Joseph—which were to continue so long as they were in the world; and as touching Abraham and his seed, out of the world they should continue; both in the world and out of the world should they continue as innumerable as the stars; or, if ye were to count the sand upon the seashore ye could not number them. This promise is yours also, because ye are of Abraham." (D&C 132:30–31.)

Conclusion

With the coming of the Father and the Son to a grove of trees in upstate New York, the light of heaven began to penetrate the long night of darkness. The fulness of the gospel of Jesus Christ was restored to the earth. And with that gospel—to be sure, as a vital part of that gospel—came also the restoration of the Abrahamic covenant. The Latter-day Saints thus enter into the ancient order of God's kingdom—they become privy to and participants in the same covenants and ordinances held sacred by the former-day Saints. In that spirit, with a knowledge that God in these last days had begun to keep his promises in regard to Abraham, Isaac, and Jacob, Elder Parley P. Pratt penned this glorious anthem in 1840:

> The morning breaks, the shadows flee;
> Lo, Zion's standard is unfurled!
> The dawning of a brighter day
> Majestic rises on the world.
>
> The clouds of error disappear
> Before the rays of truth divine;
> The glory bursting from afar
> Wide o'er the nations soon will shine.
>
> The Gentile fulness now comes in,
> And Israel's blessings are at hand.
> Lo, Judah's remnant, cleansed from sin,
> Shall in their promised Canaan stand.
>
> Jehovah speaks! Let earth give ear,
> And Gentile nations turn and live.
> His mighty arm is making bare
> His cov'nant people to receive.

Angels from heav'n and truth from earth
Have met, and both have record borne;
Thus Zion's light is bursting forth
To bring her ransomed children home.
                        (*Hymns*, 1985, no. 1.)

6

The Scattering and Gathering of Israel

Wherefore, because of their iniquities, destructions . . . shall come upon them; and they who shall not be destroyed shall be scattered among all nations. But behold, . . . when the day cometh that they shall believe in me, that I am Christ, then have I covenanted with their fathers that they shall be restored in the flesh . . . unto the lands of their inheritance.
—2 Nephi 10:6–7

"All things have their likeness, and all things are created and made to bear record of me," Jehovah said to Adam (Moses 6:63). No gospel principle bears a more fervent testimony of the manner in which men and women are reconciled to God, and in which our spirits are restored to our bodies in the resurrection, than the doctrine of the scattering and gathering of Israel (see 2 Nephi 9:1–4). Just as an individual's sins bring alienation from things of holiness, so Israel's sins separate her from the Holy One of Israel and from the people and place of covenant. And just as one is restored to the spiritual realm through repentance, so Israel is gathered—first to her God and then to the lands of her inheritance—as she forsakes and eschews the ways of the world and renews her covenant with Jesus Christ, who is its mediator.

The Scattering

Those of the house of Israel who follow the Light of Christ in this life will, either here or hereafter, be led to the covenant gospel and the higher light of the Holy Ghost; they will come to know the Lord and come unto him. In time they will come to know of their noble heritage and of the royal blood that flows through their veins. As we have shown, they have come to earth with a predisposition to receive the truth, with an inner attraction to the holy gospel. "My sheep hear my voice," the Master said, "and I know them, and they follow me" (John 10:27). "The blood of Israel has flowed in the veins of the children of men," Wilford Woodruff declared, "mixed among the Gentile nations, and when they have heard the sound of the Gospel of Christ it has been like vivid lightning to them; it has opened their understandings, enlarged their minds, and enabled them to see the things of God. They have been born of the Spirit, and then they could behold the kingdom of God." (JD 15:11.)

And, as we have sought to emphasize, chosenness implies a succession of choices. Those who became Israel before the world was, those who were *called* in that premortal existence, must exercise wisdom and prudence and discernment in this life before they can become truly *chosen* to enjoy the privilege of ruling and reigning in the house of Israel forever. The vivid and harsh reality is that lineage and ancestry alone do not qualify one for a divine family inheritance. Both the Old Testament and the Book of Mormon—and it is particularly in the latter volume that we see the pattern clearly—set forth in consistent detail the reasons why the people of Israel have been scattered and how it is they are to be gathered.

Speaking on behalf of Jehovah, Moses warned ancient Israel that if they should reject their God they would be scattered among the nations, dispersed among the Gentiles. "If thou wilt not hearken unto the voice of the Lord thy God," he said, "to observe to do all his commandments and his statutes which I command thee this day, . . . [you will be] removed into all the kingdoms of the earth. . . . And ye shall be plucked from off the land whither thou goest to possess it. And the Lord shall scatter thee among all people, from the one end of the earth even unto the other; and there thou shalt serve other gods, which neither thou nor thy fathers have known." (Deuteronomy 28:15, 25, 63–64.) The Lord spoke in a similar vein through Jeremiah more than half a millennium later: "Because your fathers have forsaken me, saith the Lord, and have walked after other gods, and have served them, and have worshipped them, and have forsaken me, and have not kept my law; and ye have done worse than your fathers; . . .

therefore will I cast you out of this land into a land that ye know not, . . . where I will not shew you favour" (Jeremiah 16:11–13). The people of God became scattered—alienated from Jehovah and the ways of righteousness, lost as to their identity as covenant representatives, and displaced from the lands set aside for their inheritance—because they forsook the God of Abraham, Isaac, and Jacob and partook of the worship and ways of unholy men.

The Book of Mormon presents the same message. In writing of the Jews, who symbolize all the house of Israel (see 1 Nephi 15:17, 20; 3 Nephi 29:8; Mormon 5:14), Jacob taught that "after [the Lord] should manifest himself they should scourge him and crucify him. . . . And after they have hardened their hearts and stiffened their necks against the Holy One of Israel, behold, the judgments of the Holy One of Israel shall come upon them," such that "they [will be] driven to and fro." In short, they "shall be scattered, and smitten, and hated." (2 Nephi 6:9–11.) Jacob later explained that "because of priestcrafts and iniquities," the Jews "will stiffen their necks against [Christ], that he be crucified. . . . And they who shall not be destroyed shall be scattered among all nations." (2 Nephi 10:5–6.)

Of course, the same warnings were sounded to the Nephites. Nephi the son of Helaman predicted that unless the Nephites turned from their wickedness, the God of Israel would, instead of gathering his people, scatter them (see Helaman 7:19). In summary, then, why was Israel scattered? Elder Bruce R. McConkie responded:

> The answer is clear; it is plain; of it there is no doubt. Our Israelite forebears were scattered because they rejected the gospel, defiled the priesthood, forsook the church, and departed from the kingdom. They were scattered because they turned from the Lord, worshipped false gods, and walked in all the ways of the heathen nations. They were scattered because they forsook the Abrahamic covenant, trampled under their feet the holy ordinances, and rejected the Lord Jehovah, who is the Lord Jesus, of whom all the prophets testified. Israel was scattered for apostasy. (*New Witness*, p. 515.)

We hasten to add that although Israel is almost always scattered because of her apostasy, there are times when the Lord scatters or leads away certain branches of his chosen people to the nethermost parts of the earth in order to accomplish his purposes—to spread the blood and influence of Abraham throughout the globe. Through this means, all the families of the earth will be blessed eventually, either through being of the blood of Abraham themselves or through being ministered to by the blood of Abraham, with the right to the gospel, the priesthood, and eternal life (Abraham 2:8–11). Sometimes the Omniscient One will, because of the waywardness of the nation in which a branch of Israel lives (or the spiritual leaders or "pastors" who have failed in their duties), lead away groups of people from among the perversion of a sinful world. From the more perfect rendering of Isaiah's oracle as contained on the brass plates, we read: "Hearken, O ye house of Israel, all ye that are broken off and are driven out because of the wickedness of the pastors of my people; yea, all ye that are broken off, that are scattered abroad, who are of my people, O house of Israel" (1 Nephi 21:1). This was exactly the case with the Lehite colony, a branch of Joseph who were led away from their homeland to another hemisphere because of wickedness in the land. How appropriate, therefore, that through Jeremiah, a contemporary of Lehi, Jehovah should sound the following warning:

> Woe be unto the pastors that destroy and scatter the sheep of my pasture! saith the Lord.
>
> Therefore thus saith the Lord God of Israel against the pastors that feed my people; Ye have scattered my flock, and driven them away, and have not visited them: behold, I will visit upon you the evil of your doings, saith the Lord.
>
> And I will gather the remnant of my flock out of all countries whither I have driven them, and will bring them again to their folds; and they shall be fruitful and increase.
>
> And I will set up shepherds over them which shall feed them: and they shall fear no more, nor be dismayed, neither shall they be lacking, saith the Lord. (Jeremiah 23:1–4.)

The Book of Mormon bears a like testimony. Nephi taught: "Behold, the Lord hath created the earth that it should be inhabited; and he hath created his children that they should possess it. And he raiseth up a righteous nation, and destroyeth the nations of the wicked. And he leadeth away the righteous into precious lands, and the wicked he destroyeth, and curseth the land unto them for their sakes [i.e., because of their deeds]." (1 Nephi 17:36–38.) Or even more plainly, Jacob explained:

> And now, my beloved brethren, seeing that our merciful God has given us so great knowledge . . . , let us remember him, and lay aside our sins, and not hang down our heads, for we are not cast off; nevertheless, we have been driven out of the land of our inheritance; but we have been led to a better land. . . .
>
> For behold, the Lord God has led away [groups of people] from time to time from the house of Israel, according to his will and pleasure. And now behold, the Lord remembereth all them who have been broken off, wherefore he remembereth us also. (2 Nephi 10:20–22.)

In addition to themselves, the people of Lehi understood full well that the Lord could and did lead away other groups of people to America and to other lands as a part of the scattering and dissemination of that people we call Israel (see 2 Nephi 1:5).

In summary, as Elder Joseph Fielding Smith wrote in regard to the tribe of Ephraim:

> In scattering Ephraim the Lord had two purposes in mind. First, the scattering was to be a punishment to a rebellious people. Second, it was for the purpose of blessing the people of other nations with the blood of Israel among whom Ephraim "mixed" himself. The scattering of other Israelites answered the same purpose. We have very good reason to believe, however, that it was the tribe of Ephraim, rebellious, proud and headstrong, which was scattered more than any other among the people of other nations. The chief reason is that it is Ephraim who is now being gathered from among the nations. (*Utah Genealogical and Historical Magazine*, 21:2 [January 1930].)

The Gathering

In speaking of the gathering of Israel, the Prophet Joseph Smith observed: "It is a principle I esteem to be of the greatest importance to those who are looking for salvation in this generation, or in these, that may be called, 'the latter times.' All that the prophets that have written, from the days of righteous Abel, down to the last man that has left any testimony on record for our consideration, in speaking of the salvation of Israel in the last days, goes directly to show that it consists in the work of the gathering." (*Teachings*, p. 83.) By means of the gathering, people are called out of Babylon into Zion, are enabled to congregate with the faithful, and are prepared and made worthy to receive the highest of all earthly blessings, the ordinances of exaltation as delivered to the obedient in the house of the Lord.

The gathering of Israel is accomplished through repentance and turning to the Lord. Individuals were gathered in ancient days when they aligned themselves with the people of God, with those who practiced the religion of Jehovah and received the ordinances of salvation. They were gathered when they gained a sense of tribal identity, when they came to know who they were and whose they were. They were gathered when they congregated with the former-day Saints, when they settled on those lands designated as promised lands—lands set apart as sacred sites for people of promise. The hope of the chosen people from Adam to Isaac and the longing of the house of Israel from Joseph to Malachi was to be reunited with their God and to enjoy fellowship with those of the household of faith. Isaiah recorded:

> But now thus saith the Lord that created thee, O Jacob, and he that formed thee, O Israel, Fear not: for I have redeemed thee, I have called thee by thy name; thou art mine.
>
> When thou passest through the waters, I will be with thee; and through the rivers, they shall not overflow thee: when thou walkest through the fire, thou shalt not be burned; neither shall the flame kindle upon thee.
>
> For I am the Lord thy God, the Holy One of Israel, thy Saviour. . . .
>
> Since thou wast precious in my sight, thou hast been honourable, and I have loved thee: therefore will I give men for thee, and people for thy life.
>
> Fear not: for I am with thee: I will bring thy seed from the east, and gather thee from the west;
>
> I will say to the north, Give up; and to the south, Keep not back: bring my sons from far, and my daughters from the ends of the earth. (Isaiah 43:1–6.)

"Ye shall be gathered one by one, O ye children of Israel," Isaiah declared (Isaiah 27:12). The call to the dispersed of Israel has been and ever will be the same: "Turn, O backsliding children, saith the Lord; for I am married unto you: and I will take you one of a city, and two of a family, and I will bring you to Zion" (Jeremiah 3:14). That is to say, gathering is accomplished through individual conversion;

through faith, repentance, baptism, and confirmation; through receiving and obeying the ordinances of the holy temple.

Indeed, the Old Testament and the Book of Mormon prophets longed for the day when the scattered remnants of Israel—those lost to their tribal and thus covenant identity and lost to their relationship with the true Messiah and his church and kingdom—would be a part of a work that would cause all former gatherings to pale into insignificance. "Therefore, behold," Jeremiah recorded, "the days come, saith the Lord, that it shall no more be said, The Lord liveth, that brought up the children of Israel out of the land of Egypt; but, The Lord liveth, that brought up the children of Israel from the land of the north, and from all lands whither he had driven them." And how is such a phenomenal gathering to be accomplished? Jehovah answers: "Behold, I will send for many fishers, saith the Lord, and they shall fish them; and after will I send for many hunters, and they shall hunt them from every mountain, and from every hill, and out of the holes of the rocks." (Jeremiah 16:14–16.) That is, through the great missionary work of the Church, the Elders and Sisters—the Lord's legal administrators in the great proselyting and gathering program—seek out, teach, baptize, and thereby gather the strangers home.

The Book of Mormon is even more specific in clarifying this principle of gathering: the people of Israel will be gathered again to the degree that they return to Christ and become formally associated with the Saints of God. That is, people are gathered first spiritually and second temporally, first to the Lord and his Church and then to the lands of their inheritance or to the congregations of the Saints. Nephi wrote that "after the house of Israel should be scattered they should be gathered together again; or, in fine, after the Gentiles had received the fulness of the Gospel [i.e., after the Restoration through Joseph Smith had taken place], the natural branches of the olive-tree, or the remnants of the house of Israel, should be grafted in, or come to the knowledge of the true Messiah" (1 Nephi 10:14). Nephi later explained to his rebellious brothers some of their father's words concerning Israel's destiny:

> And now, the thing which our father meaneth concerning the grafting in of the natural branches through the fulness of the Gentiles, is, that in the latter days, when our seed shall have dwindled in unbelief,

yea, for the space of many years, and many generations after the Messiah shall be manifested in body unto the children of men, then shall the fulness of the gospel of the Messiah come unto the Gentiles, and from the Gentiles unto the remnant of our seed—

And at that day shall the remnant of our seed know that they are of the house of Israel, and that they are the covenant people of the Lord; and then shall they know and come to the knowledge of their forefathers, and also to the knowledge of the gospel of their Redeemer, which was ministered unto their fathers by him; wherefore, they shall come to the knowledge of their Redeemer and the very points of his doctrine, that they may know how to come unto him and be saved (1 Nephi 15:13–14; compare 2 Nephi 30:5; Mormon 7:1–10).

Jacob reminded his people that the Lord God "has spoken unto the Jews, by the mouth of his holy prophets, even from the beginning down, from generation to generation, until the time comes that they [the Jews, or the house of Israel] shall be restored to the true church and fold of God; when they shall be gathered home to the lands of their inheritance, and shall be established in all their lands of promise" (2 Nephi 9:2). The sequence of gathering—first to Christ, his Church, and the true points of his doctrine, and then to specific locations—is clear in Jacob's words. Having taught that the people of Jerusalem who reject the Savior will be "scattered among all nations," he added: "Thus saith the Lord God: When the day cometh that they shall believe in me, that I am Christ, then have I covenanted with their fathers that they shall be restored in the flesh, upon the earth, unto the lands of their inheritance" (2 Nephi 10:6–7; compare 3 Nephi 20:29–33).

These teachings in the Book of Mormon help to clarify a matter that is frequently misunderstood by members and nonmembers alike: the physical gathering of Jews from all over the world to the Holy Land is not the prophesied gathering of Judah. "Judah will gather to old Jerusalem in due course; of this there is no doubt," Elder McConkie wrote.

> But this gathering will consist of accepting Christ, joining the Church, and receiving anew the Abrahamic covenant as it is administered in holy places. The present assembling of people of Jewish ancestry into the Palestinian nation of Israel is not the scriptural gathering of Israel or of Judah. It may be prelude thereto, and some of the people so as-

sembled may in due course be gathered into the true church and kingdom of God on earth, and they may then assist in building the temple that is destined to grace Jerusalem's soil. But a political gathering is not a spiritual gathering, and the Lord's kingdom is not of this world. (*New Witness*, pp. 519–20; see also pp. 511, 564–65; *The Millennial Messiah*, p. 229.)

When the scriptures thus speak of a day when the Jews "begin to believe in Christ" (2 Nephi 30:7), they do not refer to anything other than a premillennial acceptance, by a remnant of the Jews, of Jesus of Nazareth as Lord God and Messiah of Israel. To say that they "shall begin to believe in Christ" is to indicate that some Jews shall begin to be converted to The Church of Jesus Christ of Latter-day Saints before the Second Coming in glory. A remnant of such converts to the Church shall be in place (see D&C 45:43). Thus, before the great and dreadful day of the Lord, "some of them will accept the gospel and forsake the traditions of their fathers; a few will find in Jesus the fulfillment of their ancient Messianic hopes; but their nation as a whole, their people as the distinct body that they now are in all nations, the Jews as a unit shall not, at that time, accept the word of truth. But a beginning will be made; a foundation will be laid; and then Christ will come and usher in the millennial year of his redeemed." (Bruce R. McConkie, *The Millennial Messiah*, pp. 228–29.) These are they who will have responded to the impressions of the Holy Spirit that testify that Jesus is the Christ, that Joseph Smith was called of God, and that the restored kingdom of God is once again among men. These are they who will have humbled themselves to receive baptism at the hands of legal administrators and who will have "been washed in the blood of the Lamb" (Ether 13:11) unto that new life in Christ.

In short, the restoration of Israel is primarily their restoration to the knowledge of Christ (see Mormon 9:36; 3 Nephi 20:29–33). "It is not the *place* of gathering that will save the scattered remnants," Elder Bruce R. McConkie has written, "but the *message* of salvation that comes to them in their Redeemer's name. . . . Salvation is not in a *place* but in a *person*. It is in Christ." (*The Millennial Messiah*, p. 200.) President Spencer W. Kimball likewise summarized this principle as follows: "Now, the gathering of Israel consists of joining the true church and their coming to a knowledge of the true God. . . . Any person, therefore, who has accepted the restored gospel, and who now seeks to worship the Lord in his own tongue and with the Saints in the nations where he lives, has complied with the law of the gathering of Israel and is heir to all of the blessings promised the Saints in these last days." (*Teachings of Spencer W. Kimball*, p. 439.) And so people are gathered into the fold of God through learning the doctrine of Christ and subscribing to the principles and ordinances of his gospel. They learn through scripture and through patriarchal and prophetic pronouncements of their kinship with, or in a few instances today, of their adoption into, the house of Israel.

Zion: The Place of Gathering

Zion is the place of gathering. Those who accept the true Messiah, who accept Joseph Smith and the Restoration, and who seek to unite with the true Church are gathered into the fold of the true Shepherd. The Latter-day Saints in Joseph Smith's day anticipated the complete realization of the prophesied day when "the Lord thy God will turn thy captivity, and have compassion upon thee, and will return and gather thee from all the nations" (Deuteronomy 30:3). The society of Zion was the ensign, and the converts to the faith were those who would gather to the city of holiness. There were a number of reasons for a gathering or clustering of modern Israel. First, the gathering served to establish a sense of identity and focus for a people who were often shunned or persecuted for their peculiar beliefs. The one thing that all Saints from all parts of the world could share was an identity as a people, a "nation," a remnant drawn to a central site.

Second, the gathering provided the Latter-day Saints with a broader base from which to conduct missionary activities. Israel was to be gathered to her rightful locale through acceptance and worship of the true God as taught by the true Church. "We are gathering the people as fast as we can," President Brigham Young stated. "We are gathering them to make Saints of them and of ourselves." (*JD* 9:137–38.) "Ye are called to bring to pass the gathering of mine elect," six elders were told in 1830, "for mine elect hear my voice and harden not their hearts" (D&C 29:7).

Third, modern Israel gathered to a central location to escape the perils and pull of Babylon and the coming destruction upon the wicked. A revelation received in November 1831 thus announced:

"Yea, verily I say unto you again, the time has come when the voice of the Lord is unto you: Go ye out of Babylon; gather ye out from among the nations." Those in the world who were among the Gentiles were to "flee unto Zion." (D&C 133:7, 12.) "The time is near," the Prophet warned, "when the sun will be darkened, and the moon turn to blood, and the stars fall from heaven, and the earth reel to and fro. Then, if this is the case, and if we are not sanctified and gathered to the places God has appointed, with all our former professions and our great love for the Bible, we must fall; we cannot stand; we cannot be saved; for God will gather out his Saints from the Gentiles, and then comes desolation and destruction, and none can escape except the pure in heart who are gathered." (*Teachings*, p. 71; see also p. 101.)

Fourth, the Saints gathered to a central location in order to build temples, holy houses wherein the heavens were linked to the earth and the infinite powers of heaven extended to finite man. The crowning tie to Israel comes only by the worthy reception of temple blessings through being endowed and sealed into the holy order of God. "What was the object," Joseph Smith asked, "of gathering the Jews, or the people of God in any age of the world?" He then answered: "The main object was to build unto the Lord a house whereby He could reveal unto His people the ordinances of His house and the glories of His kingdom, and teach the people the way of salvation; for there are certain ordinances and principles that, when they are taught and practiced, must be done in a place or house built for that purpose." (*Teachings*, pp. 307–8.) "Missionary work," Elder Russell M. Nelson observed, "is only the beginning" to the blessings of Abraham, Isaac, and Jacob. "The fulfillment, the consummation, of those blessings comes as those who have entered the waters of baptism perfect their lives to the point that they may enter the holy temple. Receiving an endowment there seals members of the Church to the Abrahamic Covenant." ("Thanks for the Covenant," p. 59.)

In summary, people were to gather to Zion to prepare a city of holiness on earth similar to the one enjoyed by our scriptural prototype, Enoch. "In speaking of the gathering," the Prophet explained,

> we mean to be understood as speaking of it according to scripture, the gathering of the elect of the Lord out of every nation on earth, and bringing them to the place of the Lord of Hosts, when the city of righteousness shall be built, and where the people shall be of one heart and

one mind, when the Savior comes: yea, where the people shall walk with God like Enoch, and be free from sin. The word of the Lord is precious; and when we read that the veil spread over all nations will be destroyed, and the pure in heart see God, and reign with Him a thousand years on earth, we want all honest men to have a chance to gather and build up a city of righteousness, where even upon the bells of the horses shall be written "Holiness to the Lord." (*Teachings*, p. 93.)

With the powers to gather Israel formally restored to Joseph Smith and Oliver Cowdery through the theophanies in the Kirtland Temple in 1836 (see D&C 110), the Latter-day Saints became serious about their obligations in the matter of gathering. Before the missionaries had been in Britain for ten years nearly 18,000 people had been baptized (see *Millennial Star*, 8:90 [15 October 1846]). These new members were not only counseled in matters of doctrine and religious practice but were also encouraged to gather to Zion in the United States; more than 4,700 uprooted themselves and traveled to Nauvoo, Illinois (see Arrington and Bitton, *The Mormon Experience*, p. 129). Immigration to Utah in subsequent years totaled more than 85,000 (Arrington and Bitton, p. 136). "You can serve [God] just as well anywhere else [as in the Salt Lake Valley]," President Brigham Young taught in 1855, "when it is your duty to be there. If it is not your duty to be anywhere else, if you would serve him acceptably, it must be where He calls you." (*JD* 2:253.)

By the end of the nineteenth century the leaders of the Church began to sense the need for strength in remote areas, to envision the necessity of establishing the central tent of Zion with numerous stakes being driven solidly into the soil of distant lands. That the Lord himself had anticipated such development is seen in a revelation given in December 1833. In the midst of the Missouri persecutions, the word of the Lord came to modern Israel:

> Zion shall not be moved out of her place, notwithstanding her children are scattered.
>
> They that remain, and are pure in heart, shall return, and come to their inheritances, they and their children, with songs of everlasting joy, to build up the waste places of Zion—
>
> And all these things that the prophets might be fulfilled.
>
> And, behold, there is none other place appointed than that which I have appointed . . . for the work of the gathering of my saints—

Until the day cometh when there is found no more room for them; and then I have other places which I will appoint unto them, and they shall be called stakes, for the curtains or the strength of Zion. (D&C 101:17–21.)

In 1911 the First Presidency of the Church issued the following statement regarding the gathering to a central location: "The establishment of the latter-day Zion on the American continent occasions the gathering of the Saints from all nations. This is not compulsory, and particularly under present conditions, is not urged, because it is desirable that our people shall remain in their native lands and form congregations of a permanent character to aid in the work of proselyting." (*Messages of the First Presidency* 4:222.) Some six decades later Elder Bruce R. McConkie delivered an address to the Saints in Mexico and Central America that serves as a doctrinal benchmark in the matter of gathering to Zion: "This gathering," he said, "has commenced and shall continue until the righteous are assembled into the congregations of the Saints in all nations of the earth." And then, becoming more specific, Elder McConkie pointed out that "the place of gathering for the Mexican Saints is in Mexico; the place of gathering for the Guatemalan Saints is in Guatemala; the place of gathering for the Brazilian Saints is in Brazil; and so it goes throughout the length and breadth of the whole earth. Japan is for the Japanese; Korea is for the Koreans; Australia is for the Australians; every nation is the gathering place for its own people." (Conference Report, Mexico and Central America Area Conference, August 1972, pp. 43, 45.) Subsequently President Harold B. Lee "announced that the pioneering phase of gathering was now over. The gathering is now to be out of the world into the Church in every nation." (As stated by Elder Boyd K. Packer, in *Ensign*, November 1992, p. 71.)

The Book and the Gathering

The coming forth of the Book of Mormon is described as the beginning of the gathering of Israel in the last days. It is, in a sense, one of the signs of the times. In a rather lengthy but pertinent passage from the Book of Mormon, we find these words from the Risen Lord:

> And verily I say unto you, I give unto you a sign, that ye may know the time when these things shall be about to take place—that I shall gather in, from their long dispersion, my people, O house of Israel, and shall establish again among them my Zion;
>
> And behold, this is the thing which I will give unto you for a sign—for verily I say unto you that when these things which I declare unto you, and which I shall declare unto you hereafter of myself, and by the power of the Holy Ghost which shall be given unto you of the Father, shall be made known unto the Gentiles that they may know concerning this people who are a remnant of the house of Jacob, and concerning this my people who shall be scattered by them;
>
> Verily, verily, I say unto you, when these things shall be made known unto them of the Father, and shall come forth of the Father, from them unto you;
>
> For it is wisdom in the Father that they should be established in this land, and be set up as a free people by the power of the Father, that these things might come forth from them unto a remnant of your seed, that the covenant of the Father may be fulfilled which he hath covenanted with his people, O house of Israel;
>
> Therefore, when these works and the works which shall be wrought among you hereafter shall come forth from the Gentiles, unto your seed which shall dwindle in unbelief because of iniquity;
>
> For thus it behooveth the Father that it should come forth from the Gentiles, that he may show forth his power unto the Gentiles, for this cause that the Gentiles, if they will not harden their hearts, that they may repent and come unto me and be baptized in my name and know of the true points of my doctrine, that they may be numbered among my people, O house of Israel;
>
> And when these things come to pass that thy seed shall begin to know these things—it shall be a sign unto them, that they may know that the work of the Father hath already commenced unto the fulfilling of the covenant which he hath made unto the people who are of the house of Israel (3 Nephi 21:1–7).

Stated succinctly, the people of the last days may know assuredly that the work of the Father—including gathering the house of Israel, all as a part of fulfilling his promises to Abraham, Isaac, and Jacob—has begun when they see that the Book of Mormon has come forth. As Mormon declared: "When the Lord shall see fit, in his wisdom, that these sayings [the teachings of the Book of Mormon] shall come unto the Gentiles according to his word, then ye may know that the covenant which the Father hath made with the children of Israel, concerning their restoration to the lands of their inheritance, is already beginning to be fulfilled" (3 Nephi 29:1; compare Ether 4:17).

The Book of Mormon is a vital part of the work of gathering. First, it clearly teaches the reasons for the scattering of the Lord's people and also how it is that Israel is to be gathered. It is a manual, a divine handbook for understanding these central and saving concepts. Second, the Book of Mormon is the means by which Israel is to be gathered, the instrument itself for gathering the people of the covenant. "Now, what is the instrument that God has designed for this gathering?" President Ezra Taft Benson asked. "It is the same instrument that is designed to convince the world that Jesus is the Christ, that Joseph Smith is His prophet, and that The Church of Jesus Christ of Latter-day Saints is true. It is that scripture which is the keystone of our religion. It is that most correct book which, if men will abide by its precepts, will get them closer to God than any other book. It is the Book of Mormon." (Conference Report, April 1987, pp. 107–8.)

All of scattered Israel, the ten tribes included, will be gathered as they receive and accept the witness of the Book of Mormon. In discussing the manner in which he has spoken and will yet speak to his children throughout the earth, the Lord said through Nephi:

> Wherefore, because that ye have a Bible ye need not suppose that it contains all my words; neither need ye suppose that I have not caused more to be written.
>
> For I command all men, both in the east and in the west, and in the north, and in the south, and in the islands of the sea, that they shall write the words which I speak unto them; for out of the books which shall be written I will judge the world, every man according to their works, according to that which is written.
>
> For behold, I shall speak unto the Jews and they shall write it; and I shall also speak unto the Nephites and they shall write it; and I shall also speak unto the other tribes of the house of Israel, which I have led away, and they shall write it; and I shall also speak unto all nations of the earth and they shall write it.
>
> And it shall come to pass that the Jews shall have the words of the Nephites, and the Nephites shall have the words of the Jews; and the Nephites and the Jews shall have the words of the lost tribes of Israel; and the lost tribes of Israel shall have the words of the Nephites and the Jews.
>
> And it shall come to pass that my people, which are of the house of Israel, shall be gathered home unto the lands of their possessions; and

my word also shall be gathered in one. And I will show unto them that fight against my word and against my people, who are of the house of Israel, that I am God, and that I covenanted with Abraham that I would remember his seed forever. (2 Nephi 29:10–14.)

Mormon addressed himself to all the twelve tribes of Israel as follows: "I write unto you, that ye may know that ye must all stand before the judgment-seat of Christ, . . . and also that ye may believe the gospel of Jesus Christ, which ye shall have among you; and also that the Jews, the covenant people of the Lord, shall have other witness besides him whom they saw and heard, that Jesus, whom they slew, was the very Christ and the very God" (Mormon 3:20–21).

As we shall consider in more detail in chapter 8, the lost tribes of Israel are scattered among the nations. They are as scattered as to their covenant identity as they are to their geography. They will be gathered as every other person is gathered—through hearing the gospel preached by legal administrators, accepting the scriptures that declare and proclaim that gospel, and receiving the ordinances of salvation as a means of gaining membership into the kingdom of Israel, which is The Church of Jesus Christ of Latter-day Saints. After having quoted at length from 2 Nephi 30 regarding the final gathering of Israel from among the nations, President George Q. Cannon stated:

> We say frequently that we are descendants of the house of Israel. This is undoubtedly true. . . . Our ancestors were of the house of Israel but they mingled with the Gentiles and became lost, that is, they became lost so far as being recognized as of the house of Israel, and the blood of our forefathers was mingled with the blood of the Gentile nations. We have been gathered out from those nations by the preaching of the gospel of the Son of God. The Lord has made precious promises unto us, that every blessing, and every gift, and every power necessary for salvation and for exaltation to His Kingdom shall be given unto us. (Address delivered on 12 January 1890, in *Collected Discourses* [B. H. S. Publishing, 1988], 2:2–3.)

As mentioned at the beginning of this chapter, the gathering of Israel is but a type of the atonement of our Lord and Savior Jesus Christ; as Ezekiel saw in vision, the restoration of the tribes of Israel is like flesh, sinews, and life being restored to dry and inanimate bones (see Ezekiel 37). And surely the "growing together" of the stick of Judah (Bible) and the stick of Joseph (Book of Mormon) is the means by which Israel is to be gathered in the last days, the means by which false doctrines are confounded, contentions are put down, and peace is established among the people of Israel (see 2 Nephi 3:12). Truly, "when the two nations shall run together the testimony of the two nations shall run together also," as symbolized by their scriptural records (2 Nephi 29:8).

That the Book of Mormon would serve as the major instrument for gathering Israel, establishing Zion, and preparing the sons and daughters of God to receive their Savior, is evident from a very ancient prophecy. Having looked down through the stream of time, even well beyond his own translation; having agonized at the scenes of the deluge of the earth in the days of Noah; having obtained a promise from the Almighty that the earth would never again be destroyed by water; having witnessed in vision the ministry, crucifixion, and resurrection of the Lord—having done all this, the prophet Enoch asked: "When shall the earth rest?" God then showed Enoch the dark ages of apostasy, a time when the heavens were black and silent, when a veil of darkness covered the earth. And then came the promise of the ages, the dawn of Restoration:

> And righteousness will I send down out of heaven; and truth will I send forth out of the earth, to bear testimony of mine Only Begotten; his resurrection from the dead; yea, and also the resurrection of all men; and righteousness and truth will I cause to sweep the earth as with a flood, to gather out mine elect from the four quarters of the earth, unto a place which I shall prepare, an Holy City, that my people may gird up their loins, and be looking forth for the time of my coming, for there shall be my tabernacle, and it shall be called Zion, a New Jerusalem. . . . And there shall be mine abode, and it shall be Zion, which shall come forth out of all the creations which I have made; and for the space of a thousand years the earth shall rest. (Moses 7:58, 62, 64.)

That is to say, in the last days God would bring forth the Book of Mormon. He would deliver a book of scripture to a world that had been groaning in darkness (see D&C 84:49), a world that would need the word of the Lord more desperately than its people would realize. A new book of scripture. Another Testament of Jesus Christ. And what would be the role of this sacred volume? It would bear testimony that Jesus is the Christ, the Eternal God, and this it would do to a world that had denied the divine sonship and relegated the Lord of all to the category of gifted speaker and social revolutionary. To a generation who had largely reduced the pure and profound reality of the resurrection to a metaphor, it would bear testimony of his rise from the tomb. It would be central to the establishment of righteousness in the earth, a vital guide in setting forth the doctrine of Christ—the formula whereby men and women can forsake a relativistic world and come unto Christ, be changed and captained by Christ, and in process of time be perfected in Christ.

And yet there was more. The Book of Mormon, whose primary author would be Jesus Christ, would be the means whereby good men and women everywhere, men and women of a royal lineage, would be gathered to the true church and fold of God, gathered to the lands of their inheritance. And it would be the means whereby those not of Israel, those outside the lineal descent of Abraham, Isaac, and Jacob, could be led to enter the covenant and become heirs to all the promises made to the ancient fathers. The Book of Mormon would prove to be a vital key in establishing that holy commonwealth that the scriptures call Zion and would serve an indispensible role in preparing a people to welcome the returning King of Zion, Jesus the Christ. "Men and angels are to be co-workers," Joseph Smith explained, "in bringing to pass this great work, and Zion is to be prepared, even a new Jerusalem, for the elect that are to be gathered from the four quarters of the earth" (*Teachings*, p. 84). Truly, we have scarcely begun to realize what a treasure is in our midst in the form of the Book of Mormon. What wonders it has already worked is beyond belief, and only God knows the miracles it shall yet bring to pass!

Conclusion

In spite of his anxiety about the lack of space on the small plates, Jacob chose to include a complex and otherwise rather mysterious allegory written by the ancient prophet Zenos. Jacob 5, the longest chapter by far in the entire Book of Mormon, is worthy of deep and careful study. It sets forth God's plan for Israel, the means whereby he has over the generations scattered and gathered his chosen people. Though the historical and doctrinal particulars of the allegory are not all apparent, though the Lord has not seen fit to make them all known to date, the overarching and undergirding message is clear and profound—God simply will not let Israel go! Though they wander for a time, though they squander their birthright for a season, though they stray from the covenantal loyalty that ought to characterize a kingdom of priests and a holy nation, yet the God of Israel is patient and forgiving. "How merciful is our God unto us," Jacob exults, "for he remembereth the house of Israel, both roots and branches; and he stretches forth his hands unto them all the day long." And what is Jacob's plea to Israel? "Wherefore, my beloved brethren, I beseech of you in words of soberness that ye would repent, and come with full purpose of heart, and cleave unto God as he cleaveth unto you. And while his arm of mercy is extended towards you in the light of the day, harden not your hearts." (Jacob 6:4–5.)

7

A Covenant People in Ancient America

Ye are the children of the prophets; and ye are of the house of Israel; and ye are of the covenant which the Father made with your fathers.
—3 Nephi 20:25

The testimony of holy writ is that whenever the Lord has a people that he acknowledges as his own, that acknowledgment comes in the form of a covenant. It is the concept of a covenant that binds all the books of the Bible together. The Bible story is like the popular historical novels of our day in which the saga of a family is traced from generation to generation. In order to study the Bible, we often divide its books into chapters and verses that we study in blocks or small units. We rarely get the whole thing pieced back together so that we see it as the epic family saga that it is. In so doing, we could be compared to someone so busy collecting pebbles on the beach that they fail to see the ocean. Readers of the Book of Mormon, if they have a Bible background, will immediately be aware that it purports to be a continuation of the Bible story. It is a part of the same great family saga. What perhaps we have been insensitive to is how tightly the Savior's visit and teachings as recorded in 3 Nephi fit with the Bible story. Isaiah said the book would have a familiar spirit. In fact, it is more than a familiar spirit or even a strong family resemblance. This is a case of the son exactly resembling the father in features and likeness.

Definitions

Before we begin that story, it will be helpful for us to briefly define some key words and phrases. We will define terms as the Book of Mormon writers used them.

Jew. Lehi, a descendant of Joseph through Manasseh (see Alma 10:3), considered himself to be a Jew because he was a citizen of the kingdom of Judah. He was a Jewish national. Thus the Book of Mormon writers speak of themselves and their posterity as descendants of the Jews (see 2 Nephi 30:4; 33:8; D&C 19:27).

Gentile. As used in the Bible, the word *Gentile* means "nation"—i.e., a collective body. It is used in the same manner in the Book of Mormon. As a Jew is a Jewish national, so a Gentile is a citizen of a gentile nation. Thus Joseph Smith, a pure-blooded Israelite, is referred to as a Gentile, and the gospel, it is prophesied, will be restored in a gentile nation. By this definition, Latter-day Saints are Israelite by descent but Gentile by culture. Any nation that does not have prophets at its head, revelation as its constitution, and the Messiah as its king is a gentile nation.

Remnant of Jacob. "The" remnant of Jacob is composed of the twelve tribes collectively. "A" remnant of Jacob could be any of the various scattered parts of Jacob's family. For instance, Lehi's descendants are a remnant of Jacob.

Times of the Gentiles. The period between the destruction of the kingdom of Israel after the earthly ministry of Christ and the reestablishment of that nation with Christ as its king in the Millennium is known as the times of the Gentiles. At the beginning of the Millennium, all gentile or manmade governments will be superseded by the law of the gospel with Christ as King. In that day when the gentile nations—and, sadly, many Latter-day Saints—sin against the fulness of the gospel and reject its blessings, there will come the time known as the "fulness of the Gentiles" or the "fulness of the times of the Gentiles" (see 3 Nephi 16:10–11; D&C 45:25).

Redemption of Jerusalem. To be redeemed is to be freed from Satan's dominion and power. Jerusalem will be redeemed when the law of the gospel again becomes the law of its citizens. Christ will be their King, and the citizens of that kingdom will have taken upon themselves his name in the waters of baptism, have been "washed in the blood of the Lamb" (Ether 13:11), and once again will be a covenant people.

Salvation of Our God. This phrase is introduced into the Book of Mormon by the Savior, who is quoting Isaiah (see Isaiah 52:10). It refers to the ultimate triumph of Christ. The word *salvation* as used here is a translation of the Hebrew word *yeshooaw,* and it could also have been translated "deliverance" or "victory." To see the salvation of our God is to see the triumph of Christ over all his enemies. It will include the gathering of all the tribes of Israel into one fold with the Lord's sanctuary in their midst.

A Voice to Those in Darkness

With that background, we turn to the account of Christ's visit to the Nephites as recorded in 3 Nephi. In doing so, it is a panoramic view that we seek. Our interest is to see the relationship that Christ establishes between the doctrine of covenants and the promise of salvation.

Twice during the terrible night of darkness that attested to the death of Christ in the Old World, the voice of the Redeemer spoke to those in the New World. We do not think we overstate the matter in suggesting that the world has never known a more dramatic teaching moment. The audible voice of the Lord had been heard speaking from the heavens before, but never to such an extensive and numerous audience. Generally we have not given sufficient attention to what was said on those two occasions. We will begin this study at that point.

First came a voice of warning: "Wo, wo, wo unto this people; wo unto the inhabitants of the whole earth except they shall repent; for the devil laugheth, and his angels rejoice, because of the slain of the fair sons and daughters of my people; and it is because of their iniquity and abominations that they are fallen!" (3 Nephi 9:2.) Note the language used to describe those who had been slain. They were the "fair sons and daughters of [his] people," meaning they were the seed of those with whom he had made covenant.

The recitation of the destruction of great cities followed: Zarahemla, Moroni, Moronihah, Gilgal, Onihah, Mocum, Jerusalem, Gadiandi, Gadiomnah, Jacob, Gimgimno, Jacobugath, Laman, Josh, Gad, and Kishkumen. Their destruction came because there were no righteous among them and because they had soiled themselves with the blood of the Lord's prophets and Saints. Then came the testimony, "I am Jesus Christ the Son of God. . . . I came unto my own, and my own received me not." Of those who had received him, he said, "to them have I given to become the sons of God; and even so will I to as many as shall believe on my name, for behold, by me redemption cometh, and in me is the law of Moses fulfilled." (3 Nephi 9:1–17.)

The Mosaic dispensation had now ended. The old covenant had been fulfilled. Thus the instruction: "Ye shall offer up unto me no more the shedding of blood; yea, your sacrifices and your burnt offerings shall be done away, for I will accept none of your sacrifices and your burnt offerings." Foreshadowing the new order or covenant, he said: "Ye shall offer for a sacrifice unto me a broken heart and a contrite spirit. And whoso cometh unto me with a broken heart and a contrite spirit, him will I baptize with fire and with the Holy Ghost." (3 Nephi 9:19–20.) So great was the astonishment caused by this unique communication from heaven that there was silence in the land for the space of many hours. Even the wailing over the lost kindred and loved ones ceased.

A second time from the midst of the darkness the voice of the Lord was heard:

> O ye people of these great cities which have fallen, who are descendants of Jacob, yea, who are of the house of Israel, how oft have I gathered you as a hen gathereth her chickens under her wings, and have nourished you.
>
> And again, how oft would I have gathered you as a hen gathereth her chickens under her wings, yea, O ye people of the house of Israel, who have fallen; yea, O ye people of the house of Israel, ye that dwell at Jerusalem, all ye that have fallen; yea, how oft would I have gathered you as a hen gathereth her chickens, and ye would not.
>
> O ye house of Israel whom I have spared, how oft will I gather you as a hen gathereth her chickens under her wings, if ye will repent and return unto me with full purpose of heart.
>
> But if not, O house of Israel, the places of your dwellings shall become desolate until the time of the fulfilling of the covenant to your fathers. (3 Nephi 10:4–7.)

This lament is familiar to the reader of the New Testament (see Matthew 23:37), though this is an expanded version of it. It has meaning only in the context of the covenant made to the fathers. It certifies the speaker as the Messiah. None else has power to gather Israel, and none else is under covenant to do so. The burden of the message is: Because of their family ties, and because their fathers were the children of Jacob, they were gathered and nourished. Had other branches of the family been equally willing, they too would have been gathered and blessed in a like manner. The refrain then switched from a past to a future tense with a rhetorical question, "How oft will I gather you if you will repent and return to me?" Then came the warning, a very believable warning, to those to whom the Lord spoke: If you refuse spiritual fidelity, if you are not my sons and daughters according to the terms of the covenant, if you have no claim to an inheritance either temporally or spiritually, your dwelling places will be desolate "until ye have received from the hand of the Lord a just recompense for all your sins" (JST Luke 13:36). Following these words, the weeping and howling for those who had been lost again filled the darkness of the night. Mormon, who was writing the account of these things, observed at this point that Jacob had prophesied concerning a remnant of Joseph. He asked, "Are not we a remnant of the seed of Joseph? And these things which testify of us, are they not written upon the plates of brass?" (3 Nephi 10:17.)

Christ Appears at the Temple

The third time in the 3 Nephi account when a voice from heaven was heard was when the Father introduced his Son to those assembled at the temple in the land Bountiful. The text itself suggests that at least several months had elapsed between the death of Christ and the destruction on the land (see 3 Nephi 8:5; 10:18; see also Bruce R. McConkie, *The Mortal Messiah* 4:307). A group of about 2,500 people—men, women, and children—were assembled (see 3 Nephi 17:25), "conversing about this Jesus Christ, of whom the sign had been given concerning his death" (3 Nephi 11:2). They were there as families. The nature of temple worship either anciently or in our own dispensation is not such that we would normally expect a family congregation of this size to be present. Perhaps a meeting or conference of some sort was being held to discuss the recent events and the three terrible days of darkness.

The unannounced and unanticipated appearance of Christ fits the pattern of Malachi's prophecy that the messenger of the covenant would suddenly come to his temple (see Malachi 3:1). In so saying, we are not suggesting that this constitutes the complete fulfillment of that prophecy, only that it fits the pattern, a pattern that we would assume would have been duplicated in Christ's visits among the other scattered remnants of Israel.

The voice from heaven attested that the glorious being descending from heaven was his Beloved Son, and all were commanded to hear him. The heavenly visitor announced himself to be the Christ, the light and life of the world. The multitude fell to the earth in reverent awe. They were then invited to come forth, each in turn, to feel the prints in his hands and in his feet so that they might know that this was indeed the "God of Israel, and the God of the whole earth, and [that he had] been slain for the sins of the world" (3 Nephi 11:14).

Calling the Twelve to Head the New Dispensation

Following this matchless experience in which each of those present became special witnesses of the reality of Christ's suffering and triumph over death, Nephi was called and given the authority to baptize them. Eleven others were also called and given the same authority. Instructions then followed relative to how that ordinance was to be performed. All capable of repentance were to be baptized. (See 3 Nephi 11:21–28.)

The reader of the Book of Mormon will be aware that baptism was not new to the Nephite nation. Easily the greatest discourse on the subject in holy writ was penned by Nephi, the son of Lehi, nearly six hundred years earlier (see 2 Nephi 31). Why, then, would a second baptism be necessary? The text does not answer this question. It is clear, however, that the old covenant, namely the law of Moses, had come to an end. This was a new day, and a new order of things was now being introduced. The appearance of Christ, with his renewal of authority, formally constituted a new gospel dispensation among the Nephites. It was a time of new beginnings, and all were invited to claim anew their birthright in the household of faith.

Thus the Twelve were called to stand at the head of the new covenant or dispensation, again following the Old World pattern. Their number is significant, and that significance would not have been lost on either the Twelve or the multitude. The action is both symbolic and prophetic. Elder Bruce R. McConkie observed: "As there are twelve tribes in Israel, so there are twelve apostles for all Israel and the world; as Jehovah gave his saving truths to the twelve sons of Jacob and their seed, throughout their generations, so Jesus is placing in the hands of his twelve friends the saving truths and powers for their day; and as the names of the twelve tribes of Israel are written on the twelve gates of the Holy Jerusalem, which shall descend from God out of heaven, so are the names of the twelve apostles of the Lamb written on the twelve foundations of the walls of that celestial city" (*The Mortal Messiah* 2:102). The call of a Quorum of the Twelve would also have been understood as a prophecy of an ultimate day when Israel, all twelve of its tribes, would again be united as one nation under their true Messiah. As long as we have twelve Apostles, the promise exists that Israel will be gathered and the promises made to the fathers will be fulfilled.

It would be difficult to overstate the importance of the Quorum of the Twelve in the destiny of the Church and kingdom of God. That importance is established in the mouths of three witnesses—the organizations instituted by Christ in Palestine, among the Nephites, and in our own dispensation. In each instance the foundation of the Church is the Quorum of the Twelve Apostles. There are always those would-be leaders and self-ordained prophets who attempt to break with the order instituted by the Savior. Their claim is predictable enough—the Brethren are in a state of apostasy, while they themselves just happen to be the ones mighty and strong who will, according to prophecy, enter the scene just in time to save us all. What ought not be lost on us is that such claims violate the covenant made to the fathers in both a symbolic and a literal sense. The Twelve have the keys that govern the performance of the ordinance of baptism, whereby all others become heirs of the covenant of salvation. True ministers always come with the ordinances of salvation. They are always covenant spokesmen.

In the New World version of the Sermon on the Mount, given at the temple in Bountiful, the first beatitude, the one upon which all the others rest, stresses the need for sustaining the Twelve. The second is the covenant of baptism by the authority given to the Twelve. The revelations of our dispensation build on this pattern. Note the following language from the Doctrine and Covenants:

> The Twelve shall be my disciples, and they shall take upon them my name; and the Twelve are they who shall desire to take upon them my name with full purpose of heart.
> And if they desire to take upon them my name with full purpose of heart, they are called to go into all the world to preach my gospel unto every creature.
> And they are they who are ordained of me to baptize in my name, according to that which is written;
> And you have that which is written before you [having reference to the very things we are reading in 3 Nephi]; wherefore, you must perform it according to the words which are written. (D&C 18:27–30.)

This places all that follows in Christ's discourse to the Nephites in the context of covenant worthiness.

Some have tripped over the fact that those called in the New World were referred to as disciples rather than Apostles. Note that in the revelation just cited, the emphasis is similar to that in the Book of Mormon. It centers on the idea of "the Twelve" rather than on that of disciples or Apostles. One commentator observes: "They were twelve, and were accordingly known as 'the twelve.' It is doubtful whether it is proper to supply such a substantive as 'disciple' or 'apostles.' There is authority in the New Testament for the use of both of these phrases, but it does not follow that the name first given to this innermost circle of our Lord's adherents was 'the twelve disciples' or 'the twelve apostles' rather than 'the Twelve.' " (James Hastings, *Dictionary of Christ and the Gospels* 1:105.) Joseph Smith assured us, however, that those in the New World were Apostles in the full sense of the word. He taught that the order on this hemisphere was the same, the offices the same, the priesthood the same, the ordinances the same, and the gifts and powers the same as were enjoyed on the Eastern hemisphere (see *History of the Church* 4:538).

The Old World version of this sermon has too often been interpreted as an ethical discourse given by a great teacher in the community. The Book of Mormon counterpart makes it plain that these are the Messiah's words spelling out the great doctrines of the kingdom or the conditions of the covenant. This variance stands as a classic illustration of the plain and precious things that have been taken from the Bible.

Blessings are then promised those who believe the testimony of the multitude who had handled and seen the Messiah. The gift of the Holy Ghost and a remission of sins were then promised to those believers as a result of their having entered the covenant of baptism and having received the companionship of the Holy Ghost.

In the New World beatitudes, those who "give heed" to the words of the Twelve and are baptized by their authority are promised that they will receive the companionship of the Holy Ghost. More blessed still, we are told, are those who will accept the testimony of the Apostles without having seen Christ. These too are promised a remission of sins and the companionship of the Holy Ghost after their baptism. The doctrine of baptism and sustaining the Twelve places all that follows in the context of a covenant between Christ and those who bear his name.

The Covenant Sermon

Further emphasizing the idea of a new day and a new covenant, the Savior said: "Therefore those things which were of old time, which were under the law, in me are all fulfilled. Old things are done away, and all things have become new" (3 Nephi 12:46–47). Notwithstanding this statement, some were still unclear as to the fulfillment of the law of Moses. "Marvel not that I said unto you that old things had passed away, and that all things had become new. Behold, I say unto you that the law is fulfilled that was given unto Moses. Behold, I am he that gave the law, and I am he who covenanted with my people Israel; therefore, the law in me is fulfilled, for I have come to fulfill the law, therefore it hath an end." (3 Nephi 15:3–5.)

Then comes the assurance:

> Behold, I do not destroy the prophets, for as many as have not been fulfilled in me, verily I say unto you, shall all be fulfilled.
>
> And because I said unto you that old things have passed away, I do not destroy that which hath been spoken concerning things which are to come.

> For behold, the covenant which I have made with my people is not all fulfilled; but the law which was given unto Moses hath an end in me.
>
> Behold, I am the law, and the light. Look unto me, and endure to the end, and ye shall live; for unto him that endureth to the end will I give eternal life.
>
> Behold, I have given unto you the commandments; therefore keep my commandments. And this is the law and the prophets, for they truly testified of me. (3 Nephi 15:6–10.)

Turning his attention again to the Twelve, Jesus said: "Ye are my disciples; and ye are a light unto this people, who are a remnant of the house of Joseph. And behold, this is the land of your inheritance; and the Father hath given it unto you." (3 Nephi 15:12–13.)

Other Sheep

At this point in his discourse, Christ linked those of the New World with their counterparts in the Old: "Ye are they of whom I said: Other sheep I have which are not of this fold; them also I must bring, and they shall hear my voice; and there shall be one fold, and one shepherd." The Savior explained that people in the Old World had not understood what he meant when he spoke of "other sheep." Their failure to understand, he said, was the result of "stiffneckedness," "unbelief," and "iniquity." This is an instructive note explaining why so many are not able to understand the words of the Savior today. (3 Nephi 15:15–21.)

The Savior further indicated that if those in the Old World were to ask, having first made the proper spiritual preparations to receive, they could by the Holy Ghost obtain a knowledge of the lost remnants of their family. In either case, the Nephites were commanded to make a record of those sayings so that they might go forth to the believing among the Gentiles in a future day (see 3 Nephi 16:4). Those of the Old World had supposed that Christ was referring to the Gentiles in his reference to "other sheep." This indicates that they did not fully understand the implications of the Abrahamic covenant. In the divine economy of things, those of Israel were to be accorded the privilege of his personal appearance while others were to obtain their assurance of saving truths by and through the Holy Ghost. This divine timetable, Christ said, was put in place by the will of the Father (see 3 Nephi 15:15–24).

The Covenant Meal and the Sacrament

What we have traditionally supposed to be the ordinance of sacrament is recorded in chapters 18 and 20 of 3 Nephi. Though the ordinance known to us as the sacrament of the Lord's Supper was introduced by the Savior to the Nephites on these occasions, a careful reading suggests that something more was taking place.

The purpose of the sacrament is the renewal of the covenant of baptism. Earlier in the day's activities, the Savior had called the Twelve and commissioned them to baptize, or rebaptize as the case might be, all who sought membership in the Church and kingdom of God. At this point, however, none of them had been thus baptized. Their baptisms would have to wait until after the Savior's three-day ministry. (The Twelve were baptized between his first and second visits, but there is no indication that anyone else was.)

Note that the administration of the sacrament also preceded the Savior's formal conferral of authority on the newly called Twelve. A third peculiarity of these two sacrament services is the emphasis given to the fact that all present made a meal of the bread and wine. This is particularly clear in the first instance. When we have asked classes what the implications of this are, they have been quick to respond that it means they were filled with the Spirit. Yes, they had already heard the audible voice of God introduce his Son from heaven, witnessed the descent of the Son of Man, heard him testify of his divine sonship, witnessed the appearance of angels and a circling flame of fire, witnessed mass healings, and had their children blessed. To suppose that they had not yet been filled with the Spirit is inconceivable. In the instance of the first sacrament service, the Savior sent the Twelve to get bread and wine (see 3 Nephi 18:1). In the second instance he miraculously provided it (see 3 Nephi 20:6–7). This is obviously a New World counterpart of his feeding of the multitude in the Old World. The number present on this occasion is unknown, but was presumably far in excess of the 2,500 who had been in attendance the previous day.

There obviously would have been a need for physical nourishment—if not for the adults, certainly for the children. Consider the time it would take for approximately 2,500 people to personally handle and feel the wounds in the Savior's hands and feet. For each of them to have shared ten seconds with the Savior would have consumed nearly seven hours!

In the context of the covenant traditions of Israel, then, it seems that this was a covenant meal after the pattern of the one recorded in Exodus 24, where Moses, Aaron, Nadab, Abihu, and the seventy princes or elders of Israel went up on the side of Sinai (symbolically the holy place) and there saw God and "did eat and drink." This text is almost universally understood as referring to the eating of a covenant meal by the representatives of Israel in the presence of God on the holy mountain. (See E. W. Nicholson, "The Interpretation of Exodus XXIV 9–11," *Veta Testamentum*, vol. 24, no. 1 [January 1974], p. 84.) One commentary notes: "By means of the meal, Yahweh takes the whole community, represented by the clan elders, into his family. The meal is the assurance and support given by the superior, Yahweh, to the inferior, Israel." (Dianne Beragant and Robert J. Karris, ed., *Collegeville Bible Commentary*, p. 104.) The idea of two parties eating and drinking together to formally ratify a covenant is common to both the Bible and the customs of the ancient near East (see *The Bible Knowledge Commentary: Old Testament* 2:146). To eat together was to be bound together by mutual obligation (see *Harper's Bible Dictionary*, p. 616). The meal was a seal of the alliance whereby "the weaker is taken into the family of the stronger," who provides the meal (Dennis J. McCarthy, *Treaty and Covenant*, p. 254).

The two occasions have obvious similarities. The place of the meal in both cases is the temple or the holy mount (which represents the temple). Both meals are in the presence of the God of Israel. The occasion in both instances is the introduction of a new gospel dispensation. Symbolically both represent a ratifying seal of the covenant they have made. After Christ's three-day ministry among the Nephites, it appears that the more traditional sacrament observance became the order of the day. Indeed, we read that Christ continued to appear on many occasions to break bread and bless it for them (see 3 Nephi 26:13).

The Day of the Gentiles

Perhaps no part of Christ's instruction to the Nephites relative to the promises of the covenant and the events of the last days has been more misunderstood than what he said about the days of the Gentiles. Let us see if we can sort these things out.

Taking the meridian of time as a starting point, the gospel was preached first to the Jews and thereafter to the Gentiles. In our dispensation, the dispensation of the fulness of times, the gospel was, according to prophecy, brought forth by cultural Gentiles who in turn will take it to all the nations of the earth. After the gentile nations have had ample opportunity to receive it and then turn on it in wickedness, it will be taken from them and given back to its original stewards. Thus, the first shall be last and the last first (see 1 Nephi 13:42.)

When we speak of the day of the Gentiles being fulfilled, we are speaking of that time when "the consumption decreed" will make "a full end of all nations" (D&C 87:6), and a Messianic kingdom will be established in their stead. With the millennial kingdom thus established, the great work of gathering all the tribes of Israel will continue until Jacob's children enjoy that glory and power of which King David and King Solomon's days were but a type and shadow (see 3 Nephi 21:13–18; 22).

Three times the Savior refers to the words of Micah relative to the remnant of Jacob, which is to be "among the Gentiles in the midst of many people as a lion among the beasts of the forest, as a young lion among the flocks of sheep: who, if he go through, both treadeth down, and teareth in pieces, and none can deliver" (Micah 5:8; 3 Nephi 16:15; 20:16; 21:12). Interpretations of this are plentiful. Typically, they have the Lamanites purging the unworthy from the Church. In fact, the prophecy was directed to all the remnants of Israel, not a single remnant. Furthermore, the censuring is to be among "all the nations of the Gentiles," not just those in the New World. According to the words of Christ in 3 Nephi 21:12–19 (quoting Micah 5:8–14), the rending of the Gentiles—this metaphor of a lion among the sheep—takes place in a day when such things as witchcrafts, soothsayers, idolatry, immorality, priestcrafts, lying, and deceit are all destroyed and done away. When will such things be done away? Clearly, after the Lord comes and the millennial day has begun. It would seem that the image of the remnant of Israel rending its Gentile enemies is symbolic of Israel's ultimate victory over its foes, a victory that comes when the Savior returns and the wicked are destroyed. (See Bruce R. McConkie, *The Millennial Messiah*, pp. 242, 248; *The Mortal Messiah* 4:334–35.)

This warning, as it is given in chapter 16 of 3 Nephi, may be directed at the United States and those who were members of the Church and who have drifted from it. It invites the Gentiles to "return" to the Lord and speaks of those who fail to do so as "salt that hath lost its savor," thus intimating that a covenant had once been made (D&C 101:39–40). Chapter 20 speaks in the broader context of all the house of Israel and all the nations of the earth. It then speaks of the New Jerusalem that is to be built in the Americas. It intimates that all the land will be a New Zion or New Jerusalem (see 3 Nephi 20:22; Bruce R. McConkie, *The Millennial Messiah*, p. 301). In this chapter, the Savior reminds the Nephites that they are the children of the prophets, are of Israel, and are rightful heirs of the covenant. It further notes that in and through them all the families of the earth are to receive the blessings of the gospel (3 Nephi 20:27).

In chapter 21 the Lord promises a sign whereby the things he has promised might be confirmed. The sign includes the establishment of a free people in the United States of America, the restoration of the gospel, the coming forth of the Book of Mormon, the martyrdom of the Prophet Joseph Smith, and the eternal triumph of truth in the last days. The Master declares that those who reject the testimony of Joseph Smith and the Restoration, including the Book of Mormon, will, as Moses promised, "be cut off" from the Lord's people, meaning they will be left without root or branch in the eternities to come (see 3 Nephi 21:1–11).

Seeing the Salvation of Our God

Third Nephi could be viewed as a type and shadow of Christ's coming. It establishes the pattern. First will come the destruction of the wicked, those who have rejected the prophets and who have the blood of the Saints on their hands. Then, as Malachi prophesied, the Savior will come suddenly to his temple, where he will greet his covenant people. Here the assurance will again be given that the promises made to the fathers will all be fulfilled and the ancient covenant renewed. At this time, all gentile governments will end and the day of the Jew will begin. In the Millennium, the great gathering of Israel will commence in earnest as the Lost Tribes are gathered into the fold. The children of Judah will also join the Church, coming from all nations even to the extent that the children of the desolate wife, in Isaiah's imagery, will outnumber the children of the married wife; that is, those who return to the faith of their fathers will far outnumber those who are then numbered among the fold of God. Thus, it will be necessary to enlarge the place of Israel's tent, to lengthen the cords and strengthen the stakes. (See 3 Nephi 21:23–29; 22.)

Understanding the Promises Given to the Covenant People in 3 Nephi

Third Nephi contains some key passages relative to the promises of the Lord to the house of Israel. We have particular reference to chapters 16, 20, and 21. These passages have been misunderstood and misused. Often this happens innocently, sometimes not. Unstable views frequently strain the meaning of these texts to justify speculative or personally aggrandizing views. To that end, perhaps these observations ought to be made:

1. The Book of Mormon came forth to gather Israel—all Israel, not a particular or exclusive part of Israel. On its title page, Moroni stated one purpose of the book as being "to show unto the remnant of the House of Israel what great things the Lord hath done for their fathers; and that they may know the covenants of the Lord, that they are not cast off forever." Note that the emphasis is on "the" remnant of Israel, not "a" remnant. Long before Christ visited the Nephites, Israel had been scattered throughout the earth (see 1 Nephi 22:4). Christ thus announced to the Nephites that there were still others that the Father had commanded him to visit. All these scattered remnants of Jacob have claim on the promises made to their fathers. Each is "a remnant of Jacob"; collectively they are "the remnant." We can be confident that the same promises given to the remnant of Jacob in the Americas were also given to the rest of Jacob's children, wherever they may have been when the resurrected Christ visited them.

2. These chapters cannot be properly understood in isolation from the rest of the covenant sermon. They assume an understanding of the call and ordination of the Twelve (see 3 Nephi 18:36; Moroni 2:2). The whole idea of there being *twelve* instead of some other number is their symbolic representation of the twelve tribes of Israel. The

unity with which they stand at the head of the Church was and is to be a constant reminder of the Lord's promise to unite all of Israel in his millennial kingdom. The gathering of Israel and building of Zion must take place under their direction. Any supposed doctrines that hold that some remnant of Israel can do some portion of the gathering or of the building of Zion or the New Jerusalem independent of the direction of the Twelve—or likewise some leader who comes on the scene to do some marvelous thing independent of their direction—is out of harmony with the covenant of baptism and the covenant to sustain the Twelve, with which the Savior began his instruction to the Nephites (see 3 Nephi 12:1).

It ought also be observed that the same pattern and principle exists in our dispensation. The keys of the gathering of Israel and the building of Zion rest with the First Presidency, the Twelve, and none others. The Church is governed by modern revelation, not the writings of ancient prophets. Isaiah may have stood at the head of the Church in his day, but he does not stand at the head of the Church in ours. The Book of Mormon unlocks the book of Isaiah, not the other way around.

3. Spiritual stability and sound understanding are not found in strained phrases. We ought to be inherently suspicious of interpretations that aggrandize a particular group or some marvelous or mighty leader that is going to come onto the scene to straighten out the Church. The Book of Mormon, if we study it carefully, suggests that we avoid such narrow interpretations (see, for example, 1 Nephi 15:17, 20; 3 Nephi 29:8; Mormon 5:14). The Twelve are in place. Some have argued that the phrase "the arm of the Lord" has reference to a special servant of the Lord who is to come on the scene and save the day when present leaders fall short of their calling. It rather strains the idea of "the arm of the Lord" to suppose that it no longer needs to be attached to the body. In the realm of our experience, arms are always appendages to a body and not separate entities that operate without it. Nor is it reasonable to suppose that the keys given the Twelve will be taken from them or surrendered by them to some individual who supposes himself to be the one mighty and strong called to set the Church in order.

4. Wisdom suggests moderation and caution in scriptural interpretation. When these Book of Mormon chapters were discussed with Elder Bruce R. McConkie, he suggested that there were things con-

tained in them that the Lord had not chosen to make plain at the present time. It would be unwise for us to attempt to clarify what the Lord or his covenant spokesmen have not. In writing on these chapters, Elder McConkie observed: "It is not always possible for us in our present state of spiritual enlightenment to put every event into an exact category or time frame." He also noted that some of these texts "apply to both pre- and post-millennial events; some have an initial and partial fulfillment in our day and shall have a second and grander completion in the days ahead." (*The Millennial Messiah*, p. 251.)

5. In recent times we have been warned about false views relative to the gathering. The warning was specifically against "cults" and "colonies." (See Boyd K. Packer, *Ensign*, November 1992, p. 73.) The caution was to beware of those who think themselves a part of some inner circle whose understanding is ahead of those called to hold the keys of the gathering of Israel and thus to preside over all that takes place relative to it.

Conclusion

Moroni told Joseph Smith that the "fulness of the everlasting Gospel" was to be found in the instruction given by the Savior to the Nephites (see Joseph Smith—History 1:34). This message of Christ, as recorded, centers in the blessings and obligations of a covenant people. "Ye are the children of the prophets," Christ told them, "and ye are of the house of Israel; and ye are of the covenant which the Father made with your fathers, saying unto Abraham: And in thy seed shall all the kindreds of the earth be blessed" (3 Nephi 20:25).

Subject to their living righteous lives, the chosen seed of Abraham have the promise that they will be endowed with the fulness of all gospel blessings. Such is their right by birth. It is the obligation of those so endowed to carry those same blessings of salvation to all others so that all "the kindreds of the earth might be blessed." In accordance with that covenant, Christ endowed the Nephites with the fulness of his gospel and the promise that in and through them all nations of the earth would be blessed. This becomes literally so as their testament or record of Christ in the form of the Book of Mormon goes forth in these last days to gather the honest in heart out of all nations. That gathering, as the Book of Mormon attests, will be to the covenants of salvation that bring with them the fulness of all gospel blessings.

We too are the seed of Abraham and as such are heirs of the same promises and thus recipients of the same obligations as the faithful Saints have been in all ages. Like our ancient counterparts, we have been blessed with the fulness of the gospel and the obligation to declare it among all nations and peoples. As ours is the God of our fathers, so ours is the gospel of our fathers. Their hearts were turned to us and ours turn to them. Their covenant is our covenant, and their testimony becomes our testimony as we boldly declare the message of the Book of Mormon to all the nations of the earth.

8

A Scriptural Search for the Ten Tribes

Moses appeared before us, and committed unto us the keys of the gathering of Israel from the four parts of the earth, and the leading of the ten tribes from the land of the north.
—D&C 110:11

Judaism and historical Christianity both provide marvelous case studies for the process by which tradition supplants revelation and is elevated to the status of doctrine. What of Mormonism? Do we face the same danger? Do Latter-day Saints commonly teach as doctrine things for which there is little scriptural evidence? It appears that some of us do. Along with those would-be doctrines that have no roots in scripture are those others that also have been grafted into the tree of life. It is important that we separate the wheat from the chaff. One cannot make good bread with chaff, and certainly not the bread of life.

Elder Harold B. Lee explained:

> It is not to be thought that every word spoken by the General Authorities is inspired, or that they are moved upon by the Holy Ghost in everything they speak and write. Now you keep that in mind. I don't care what his position is, if he writes something or speaks something that goes beyond anything that you can find in the standard works, unless that one be the prophet, seer, and revelator—please note that one exception—you may immediately say, "Well, that is his own idea!" And

if he says something that contradicts what is found in the standard works (I think that is why we call them "standard"—it is the standard measure of all that men teach), you may know by that same token that it is false, regardless of the position of the man who says it. ("The Place of the Living Prophet, Seer, and Revelator.")

The matter is not easily resolved, but there is much that we can do to lessen the difficulties. We should remember that it is the system of heaven to dispense its treasures line upon line, precept upon precept. This means that our generation ought to be able to build upon the doctrinal understanding of previous generations; if we are continuing the journey they started, we ought to be a bit closer to the top of Mount Zion and our view ought to be a bit better. If we are to avoid becoming like the scribes and Pharisees we must do more than quote from the past. The scriptures, the spirit of revelation, and the words of our living prophet—rather than legends and traditions, however old, popular, or well received they may be—must act as our compass.

The Ten Tribes: Did They Retain Their Identity?

One common assumption among explanations as to where the ten tribes are is that the tribes have remained together as a body. Those who support this idea do so primarily on the strength of quotations from past authorities. Arguments that the ten tribes retained their identity as a body can be traced to three sources: a quotation from the book of 2 Esdras in the Old Testament Apocrypha, the verses in Doctrine and Covenants section 133 that speak of the ten tribes returning with their prophets at their head, and the statement in 3 Nephi 16 that Christ would visit the lost tribes. Let us examine each.

Second Esdras (or 4 Ezra, as it is sometimes known) may well be the most often quoted apocryphal text in Mormon literature. It has been quoted approvingly in many LDS sources, frequently by people who are quoting each other, with none of them taking the time to check the reliability of the source. This is the stuff of which traditions are made. May we suggest that an examination of the Esdras text is in order.

Second Esdras is one of the intertestamental apocryphal books. In its present form it is believed to be a Christian writing, though the core of the work is a Jewish apocalypse commonly known as 4 Ezra.

It is generally believed that its first two chapters are of Christian authorship, having been written in the second century A.D.; chapters 3–13, or the Apocalypse of Ezra, are believed to have been written toward the end of the first century A.D., and the two concluding chapters to have been written by a third-century Christian writer.

The apocalypse is set in Babylon in the thirtieth year after the destruction of Jerusalem (557 B.C.). It is ascribed to a certain Salathiel (Shealtiel), who was the father of Zerubbabel, the builder of the Second Temple (see Ezra 3:2; 1 Chronicles 3:17). In 4 Ezra, however, Salathiel identifies himself as Ezra the scribe (3:1). This places him more than a century out of time sequence! A modern equivalent would be Hyrum Smith claiming that he was also Ezra Taft Benson. Most scholars, of course, regard 4 Ezra as a fictional work, but we ought to draw our own conclusions. It contains a series of seven visions, primarily conversations with an angel, which are granted to Salathiel or Ezra in response to his prayers. His prayers, however, are more of a complaint than a petition, and his dialogue with the angel more of a disputation than the anticipated setting in which a prophet reverently receives instruction from a heavenly messenger. The spirit of the whole thing is clearly rather strange.

The text referring to the lost tribes comes in an explanation of a night dream in which Ezra sees the figure of a man coming forth out of the heart of a storm-tossed sea. The man then flies with the clouds of heaven; all that he looks upon trembles, and when he speaks all that hear his voice are consumed with fire. From the four quarters of the earth a multitude of men gather to wage war against him. He then carves for himself a great mountain and flies upon it. From his mountain he annihilates the hostile host with a stream of fire and tempest which proceeds from his mouth. The man then descends the mountain and summons to his side all who have not attempted to oppose him. (See 4 Ezra 13:1–13.)

The interpretation of the dream is that the man from the sea is the Messiah, his enemies are the nations of the world, and the graven rock is the heavenly Jerusalem that has come down to earth. The annihilation of the hostile forces is effected by the fire of the law, meaning the Law of Moses. Then the Messiah gathers the ten tribes out of alien lands, joins them with those who are already in Palestine, and establishes his millennial kingdom of peace and glory. (See 4 Ezra 13:21–39.) Our oft-quoted passage reads as follows:

> These are the ten tribes which were led away from their own land into captivity in the days of King Hoshea, whom Shalmaneser the king of the Assyrians led captive; he took them across the river, and they were taken unto another land.
>
> But they formed this plan for themselves, that they would leave the multitude of the nations and go to a more distant region, where mankind had never lived,
>
> And there at least they might keep their statutes which they had not kept in their own land.
>
> And they went in by the narrow passages of the Euphrates River.
>
> For at that time the Most High performed signs for them, and stopped the channels of the river until they had passed over. Through that region there was a long way to go, a journey of a year and a half; and that country is called Arzareth [Heb. for "another land"].
>
> Then they dwelt there until the last times; and now, when they are about to come again,
>
> The Most High will stop the channels of the river again, so that they may be able to pass over. Therefore you saw the multitude gathered together in peace.
>
> But those who are left of your people, who are found within my holy borders, shall be saved.
>
> Therefore when he destroys the multitude of the nations that are gathered together, he will defend the people who remain. And then he will show them very many wonders. (4 Ezra 13:40–49.)

There are, for the Latter-day Saint, some serious theological difficulties with the account of the millennial era as described in the book of 4 Ezra. Chief among them is the announcement that the Messiah, having ruled for four hundred years, will then die (see 7:28–29). Another is the announcement that those who are gathered in the last days will be those to whom the Lord will have shown no signs and who "have seen no prophets" (1:36–37). Yet signs of the times are given, including "women with child" who "shall give birth to premature children at three or four months, and these shall live and dance" (6:21–22). We are also told that children born of older women will not grow to the same stature as those born of younger women and that those of the last days will not be as large as those of earlier ages (see 5:53–55).

Other matters that should at least raise an eyebrow include the declaration that our sovereign Lord created the earth "without help" (3:4), that Adam was a man "burdened with an evil heart" (3:21), that "it would have been better if the earth had not produced Adam, or else, when it had produced him, had restrained him from sinning" (7:116–17), and that God does "not grieve over the multitude of those who perish . . . for they are set on fire and burn hotly, and are extinguished" (7:61).

This is a sampling of the doctrines taught in this book; we submit that it is not a good source. It could be argued that the passage referring to the ten tribes is good while the rest of the book is bad, and perhaps this is so. If we are to maintain that the ten tribes passage is a pearl found in a coal pit, it stands sorely in need of verification from a source known to be genuine, but what it cannot be is the foundation upon which the rest of our reasoning is based.

Indeed, we have no scriptural text that tells us that the ten tribes are located somewhere as a body. While it is true that Christ visited them in a group or groups in the meridian of time (see 3 Nephi 17:4), it takes a two thousand-year leap to suppose that they have remained so today. The Nephites were also in a group with prophets at their head, but no one would argue that they have retained their identity to this day. Section 133 of the Doctrine and Covenants speaks of a future day when the tribes of Israel will return under the direction of their prophets to receive a blessing at the hands of Ephraim (see D&C 133:25–32). This revelation does not, however, say that they are presently in that state. We can read it into the passage, but we do so without scriptural justification. Nor does this contradict Nephi's prophecy that we will some day have the records of the lost tribes. Nephi did not say that they would bring them to us, only that we would have them. He also said that we would have the words of the Nephites, the Jews, and others, but he did not say that the Nephites or the Jews would bring them to us (see 2 Nephi 29:12–14).

In spite of the fact that it has been a popular part of Mormon tradition to argue that the ten tribes are off somewhere together, the idea presents critical theological difficulties and raises a number of serious questions. How could the apostasy have been universal and not affect those of the lost tribes? And if there were no apostasy among them, why the need for a restoration? Why restore priesthood and keys that have not been lost? Why give Joseph Smith the Presidency and responsibility for events over which he has no control? And what is wrong with the priesthood authority of these prophets and their tribes that they have never sought to share its blessings with others? Is The Church of Jesus Christ of Latter-day Saints the "only true and living

Church upon the earth," as the Lord declared (D&C 1:30), or are there other true but hidden churches?

Scriptural Descriptions of the Gathering

We will respond to the other two arguments regarding the ten tribes through a series of questions and answers.

Question: What is the covenant that God made with Abraham?

Answer: We repeat that God said to Abraham, "I have purposed to take thee away out of Haran, and to make of thee a minister to bear my name in a strange land which I will give unto thy seed after thee for an everlasting possession, when they hearken to my voice" (Abraham 2:6). The covenant, then, was that Abraham would be a missionary: he would go into the land of Canaan and teach and testify that Jehovah was the only true and living God. In return, God promised to give that land to Abraham and his posterity as an "everlasting possession"; that is, it was to be the place of their abode both in this life and the next if and "when" they hearkened to his voice. Obviously, none of Abraham's seed could lay claim to such an inheritance in disobedience or rebellion.

Further, God promised Abraham that he would make of him a great nation, that he would bless him above measure, that his name would be great among all nations, and that he would be a blessing unto his seed. Of Abraham's seed the Lord said, "They shall bear this ministry." They, like Abraham, must be missionaries, bearing the name of the Lord Jehovah in strange lands. Abraham was promised that they would bear the priesthood among all nations: at the hands of his seed all families of the earth were to be blessed "with the blessings of the Gospel, which are the blessings of salvation, even of life eternal." (Abraham 2:10, 11.)

It was a spiritual covenant that God made with Abraham, a covenant centering in obedience, missionary work, the gospel of salvation, and the promise of eternal life. The great issue was not so much *where* Abraham lived, but *how* he lived. A land of inheritance is simply an earthly token and reminder of the eternal rewards awaiting those who honor their covenants. It is appropriate that if Abraham or his seed break those covenants, the token—the land promised them—would be taken from them. When they once again begin to live those covenants, then, and only then, should they be returned to that land that symbolizes their obedience.

That this principle might be written upon the hearts of Abraham's seed, God commanded that the day Israel crossed the Jordan to enter the land the Lord their God had given them, they were to proceed to the vale between Ebal and Gerizim. There the tribes were to be divided, six tribes to stand upon Mount Gerizim facing six tribes standing on Mount Ebal. The priests in the vale between the two mounts then read the blessings promised in the law. Thus Israel covenanted to receive the blessings of obedience or the cursings of disobedience with a marvelous shout of "Amen!" (See Deuteronomy 27–28; Joshua 8:30–35.) Among the curses for disobedience accepted by covenant that day was that the Lord would scatter them, all of Israel, "among all people, from the one end of the earth even unto the other," and that in their scattered state they would worship false gods and know no peace (Deuteronomy 28:64–68; Leviticus 26:33).

Question: Why was Israel scattered?

Answer: As we have explained in chapter 6, Israel was scattered because she broke her covenants. "Her young men visited the temple prostitutes of Ashtoreth, and her young women defiled themselves as harlots with the heathen. Her priests sacrificed on the altars of Baal, and Solomon himself built an altar to Molech whereon Ahaz and others sacrificed children." (Bruce R. McConkie, *The Millennial Messiah,* p. 186.) She forsook "the fountain of living waters, and hewed . . . out cisterns, broken cisterns, that can hold no water" (Jeremiah 2:13). That is, she formed false churches and ceased to be a peculiar people and a kingdom of priests. Rabbis replaced prophets, traditions replaced scripture, and ritual replaced righteousness. When Israel became as the world, the Lord allowed her to suffer and live as the world. Since the knowledge of God can be had only in righteousness, she lost that knowledge and the understanding of the covenant that God had made with her. There can be no understanding of the gathering without an understanding of the scattering.

Question: Now that Israel has been scattered, do we have any indication as to the whereabouts of the lost tribes?

Answer: On this matter we have the united testimony of the standard works. Enoch in his prophetic description of the last days spoke of "righteousness and truth" sweeping the four quarters of the earth "as with a flood," to gather out the "elect" and bring them to the New

Jerusalem (Moses 7:62). In the biblical statements we begin with Moses, the first prophet to prophesy to the nation of Israel. Moses, as we have already seen, prophesied that all the tribes of Israel would be scattered to the ends of the earth should they break that covenant that entitled them to a promised inheritance in the land of Palestine. Yet, he also prophesied of a day of gathering and restoration, the responsibility for which he placed upon the shoulders of the tribe of Joseph, or more specifically, Ephraim and Manasseh. Like the horns of unicorns, he said, they would gather the people from the ends of the earth (see Deuteronomy 33:17; 30:3). In the New Testament, Christ spoke of gathering the "elect from the four winds" (Matthew 24:31), and James addressed his epistle "to the twelve tribes which are scattered abroad" (James 1:1).

Describing this day of restoration, Isaiah said that the Lord would "assemble the outcasts of Israel, and gather together the dispersed of Judah from the four corners of the earth" (Isaiah 11:12). To Ezekiel the Lord said, "I will even gather you from the people, and assemble you out of the countries where ye have been scattered" (Ezekiel 11:17). Again he said: "I will bring them out from the people, and gather them from the countries" (Ezekiel 34:13). And still again he said, "I will take the children of Israel from among the heathen, whither they be gone, and will gather them on every side" (Ezekiel 37:21).

Mormon, in like manner, taught: "I write unto all the ends of the earth; yea, unto you, twelve tribes of Israel" (Mormon 3:18). In fact, the Book of Mormon tells us that the Three Nephites "shall minister unto all the scattered tribes of Israel, and unto all nations, kindreds, tongues and people, and shall bring out of them unto Jesus many souls" (3 Nephi 28:29). With specific reference to the lost tribes, Nephi said they had been "scattered upon all the face of the earth, and also among all nations" (1 Nephi 22:3–5). The dispersion of all the tribes of Israel is taught with unquestioned authority in 3 Nephi. Consider, for instance, these words:

> Yea, and surely shall he again bring a remnant of the *seed of Joseph* to the knowledge of the Lord their God.
> And as surely as the Lord liveth, will he *gather in* from the four quarters of the earth *all the remnant* of the seed of Jacob, *who are scattered abroad upon all the face of the earth.*

And as he hath covenanted with all the house of Jacob, even so shall the covenant wherewith he hath covenanted with the house of Jacob be fulfilled in his own due time, unto *the restoring all the house of Jacob unto the knowledge of the covenant that he hath covenanted with them.*

And then shall they know their Redeemer, who is Jesus Christ, the Son of God; and then shall they *be gathered in from the four quarters of the earth unto their own lands,* from whence they have been *dispersed;* yea, as the Lord liveth so shall it be. Amen. (3 Nephi 5:23–26, emphasis added.)

Indeed, we are told that the very purpose of the coming forth of the Book of Mormon was to "gather in, from their long dispersion" the "house of Israel" (3 Nephi 21:1), or as Moroni stated it, to gather "the ancient and long dispersed covenant people of the Lord" (Mormon 8:15; compare 3 Nephi 21:26–27).

The Lord told Joseph Smith that the Church had been organized so that He might gather the "elect from the four quarters of the earth, even as many as will believe in [him], and hearken unto [his] voice" (D&C 33:5–6). The Prophet was also told that the 144,000—twelve thousand out of each tribe—would be high priests, ordained "out of every nation, kindred, tongue, and people" upon the earth (D&C 77:11). As Joseph Smith dedicated the first temple of our dispensation, he prayed that "all the scattered remnants of Israel," whom he said had "been driven to the ends of the earth," might "come to a knowledge of the truth, believe in the Messiah, and be redeemed" (D&C 109:67). When the Prophet said that John the Revelator was with the ten tribes, he said he was "to prepare them for their return from their long dispersion, to again possess the land of their fathers" (*History of the Church* 1:176).

Question: Does Doctrine and Covenants 133 tell us that when the ten tribes return they will have their scriptural records with them?

Answer: No. Elder Bruce R. McConkie has observed that "we and they will have their scriptures; and those scriptures will tell of the visit of the Risen Lord among their forebears. How they shall be brought to light is not known. It may be in much the same way the Book of Mormon was revealed to the world." (*New Witness,* p. 521.) One further matter. It just may be that a portion of the record of the ten tribes is already in our possession. The Doctrine and Covenants is a record of God's dealings with a people who are a remnant of one of the lost tribes, even the tribe of Ephraim.

As he prophetically described the latter-day gathering of Israel to the Nephites, Christ quoted a number of verses from the book of Micah. Of special interest is Micah's imagery of returning Israel as a goring bull having horns of iron and hoofs of brass to "beat in pieces many people," this that their earthly riches might be consecrated to the Lord (3 Nephi 20:19; Micah 4:13). The passage, which is clearly millennial, might explain the statement in Doctrine and Covenants 133 that "their enemies will become a prey unto them" (v. 28). The spoils of the earth are then returned to their rightful master.

Question: Are there scriptural keys that help in interpreting the description of the returning tribes of Israel from the north countries in Doctrine and Covenants 133, specifically of such things as their smiting the rocks, the ice flowing down at their presence, a highway being cast up in the midst of the great deep, the barren deserts bringing forth pools of living water, and the parched ground becoming no more a thirsty land (vv. 26–27, 29)?

Answer: Doctrine and Covenants 133 weaves together scores and scores of phrases that come from Old Testament prophecies. In some instances it announces their fulfillment, while in others it provides additional prophecy that will surround their eventual fulfillment. The language in question here comes primarily from Isaiah 35. In fact, these verses from the Doctrine and Covenants and the Isaiah chapter need to be studied together because they clarify each other. For instance, Isaiah tells us that the highway that is to be cast up is the "way of holiness," that the "unclean shall not pass over it," but that the "redeemed," or the "ransomed of the Lord," shall walk there (Isaiah 35:8–10). It ought also to be noted that whereas the King James Bible records Isaiah saying "an highway shall be there, and a way," the Joseph Smith Translation reads, "an highway shall be there, a way *shall be cast up*" (v. 8, emphasis added). As to the quenching of the thirsty land and the springs of water that are to come forth, the Doctrine and Covenants tells us that the water that breaks forth is "living water," or, as the Savior said, "a well of water springing up into everlasting life" (John 4:14).

The major theme of both ancient and modern scripture is that no power or force can stay these events. As it was with ancient Israel, so it will be with Israel of the last days. "Behold, I say unto you," the Lord said through the Prophet Joseph Smith, "the redemption of Zion must needs come by power; therefore, I will raise up unto my people a man, who shall lead them like as Moses led the children of Israel. For ye are the children of Israel, and of the seed of Abraham, and ye must needs be led out of bondage by power, and with a stretched-out arm. And as your fathers were led at the first, even so shall the redemption of Zion be." (D&C 103:15–18.) Thus, if the ancient Moses could smite a rock and bring forth water, the modern Moses must be able to do the same. Isaiah tells us that "there shall be an highway for the remnant of his people . . . like as it was to Israel in the day that he came up out of the land of Egypt" (Isaiah 11:16). Thus Isaiah refers to a power that removes all obstacles, not to a four-lane interstate freeway. "Prepare ye the way of the people," he wrote, "cast up, cast up the highway; gather out the stones; lift up a standard for the people" (Isaiah 62:10). The image is not one of transits, shovels, and flags; ancient covenant has been restored and by his power the Lord will redeem his people (see Isaiah 62:11–12). Elder McConkie has written:

> In the literal sense of the word, the Ten Tribes will not return with armies and trumpets and banners; with the ice flowing down at their presence; on a highway spanning oceans and continents over which their legions shall march in regal majesty. Their return will be marvelous, with miracles attending. They will tread the highway of righteousness, and it will be as though a nation had been born in a day, because the wicked will have been destroyed and the Lord himself will be reigning on earth. The return of the Ten Tribes is, of course, a Millennial event. (*New Witness*, p. 521.)

Question: How, then, are we to understand the statement in Doctrine and Covenants 133 that prophets among the returning tribes will lead them?

Answer: Certainly when the time comes that the tribes of Israel return from the north countries, or for that matter from any other place, they will come with their prophets leading them. The Lord's people always have been and always will be led by prophets.

The issue here is the possibility of prophets serving independently of the priesthood and keys restored to Joseph Smith. If we are to accept the standard established in the Doctrine and Covenants, we must maintain that none have the right to act in the name of the Lord (and surely that would include leading the tribes of Israel) save they have been "ordained by some one who has authority, and it is known to the church that he has authority and has been regularly ordained by the heads of the church" (D&C 42:11). The Doctrine and Covenants accepts none in the latter days as prophets save those who have been called, ordained, and received the sustaining vote of the Church. The Lord's house is and always has been a house of order. Is it not wholly harmonious with the revelations and all we know about the Lord's system of governing his people to suppose that these prophets will be elders of Israel who trace their priesthood ordinations to Joseph Smith and Oliver Cowdery and through them to Peter, James, and John? In other words, the scattered remnants of Israel will hear the message of the Restoration preached by Mormon missionaries, will feel the witness of the Spirit and accept baptism at the hands of legal administrators, and will thereby join themselves with (gather to) the congregations and stakes of the Saints. They will be led into the fold under the direction of their prophets, meaning the quorum presidents, bishops, and stake presidents who direct the work of the kingdom in the stakes of Zion.

Question: What about Joseph Smith's statement that John the Revelator was with the ten tribes preparing them for their return? Doesn't this indicate that they are together in a body?

Answer: In the minutes of a conference of the Church held in June 1831, John Whitmer recorded as follows: "The Spirit of the Lord fell upon Joseph in an unusual manner, and he prophesied that John the Revelator was then among the Ten Tribes of Israel who had been led away by Shalmaneser, king of Assyria, to prepare them for their return from their long dispersion, to again possess the land of their fathers" (*History of the Church* 1:176). Far from saying they were in a body, the Prophet spoke of "their long dispersion." Again, if we are going to be true to the scriptures, it can be no other way. Be it remembered, and it is recorded in the book of Revelation, that the Lord told John that he "must prophesy, again before many peoples, and nations, and tongues, and kings" (Revelation 10:11). In a revealed explanation of this prophecy the Lord told Joseph Smith "that it was a mission, and an ordinance, for [John] to gather the tribes of Israel" (D&C 77:14). The Book of Mormon tells us that John's fellow laborers, the Three Nephites, were told that they would labor among every nation, kindred, tongue, and people to gather scattered Israel. The record also states that they would labor among the Jews and Gentiles and that the Jews and Gentiles would not know them (see 3 Nephi 28:27–29). That, it appears, is the pattern for John's ministry also.

Question: Why is it that our revelations speak of the gathering of Israel and the return of the ten tribes as two separate events?

Answer: Moses conferred upon the heads of Joseph Smith and Oliver Cowdery "the keys of the gathering of Israel from the four parts of the earth, and the leading of the ten tribes from the land of the north" (D&C 110:11). In the tenth article of faith, the Prophet wrote: "We believe in the literal gathering of Israel and in the restoration of the Ten Tribes." It appears that two separate events are being described. If the literal gathering of Israel embraces all twelve tribes, why then the seemingly redundant statement that the ten tribes will also be returned to their ancient lands?

The gathering comes in response to the scattering. We can quite properly consider the scattering as consisting of two parts: the leading of the ten tribes into the north countries, and the dispersing of the twelve tribes among all the nations of the earth. Thus, as the scattering can be divided into two major events, so it must be with the gathering. If there is to be a restoration of all things, the gathering of the twelve tribes must be as literal as their scattering; the ten tribes must return from the north countries as assuredly as they were taken into the north countries. Thus, after the remnants of the ten tribes have been gathered through the waters of baptism, some representative number of them will return to their ancient lands of inheritance. Nothing short of this answers the promise of a restoration of all things. Of singular importance here is the fact that both events are to take place under the direction of the President of The Church of Jesus Christ of Latter-day Saints.

Question: If we were to capsulize the message of the Book of Mormon relative to the gathering of Israel in a single sentence, what would it be?

Answer: The message of the Book of Mormon is that Israel was scattered for rejecting Christ and will be gathered only by accepting him.

Question: Do the Book of Mormon and the Doctrine and Covenants give Latter-day Saints a different perspective of the gathering than that held by the Bible-believing world?

Answer: The perspective is as different as the infant child is from the fully mature adult it will yet become. For instance, were it not for the Book of Mormon and the revelations of Joseph Smith we would not know:

1. That the resurrected Christ visited the lost tribes (see 3 Nephi 16:1–4).

2. That the lost tribes kept scriptural records of their own which someday we will be privileged to read (see 2 Nephi 29:12–14).

3. That Isaiah's prophecy relative to Zion putting on her strength and her beautiful garments referred to the restoration of the priesthood, while the prophecy of her loosing the bands of her neck referred to the receiving of revelation in the great day of restoration (see D&C 113:7–10).

4. That it was necessary for Moses to return and restore "the keys of the gathering of Israel from the four parts of the earth, and the leading of the ten tribes from the land of the north" (see D&C 110:11).

5. That both John the Revelator and the Three Nephites would, as translated beings, join us in our efforts to gather Israel (see D&C 77:14; 3 Nephi 28:25–29).

6. That there are lands of promise, including the Americas, rather than just the land of the Bible, to which Israel will be gathered (see 1 Nephi 22:12; 2 Nephi 6:11; 9:2; 10:7–8).

7. That the Jerusalem of the Old World is to be restored and a New Jerusalem is to be built upon the American continent (see 3 Nephi 20:22; Ether 13:3–13).

8. That the fulness of the gospel as restored through Joseph Smith is "the covenant" or testament that God "sent forth to recover [his] people, which are of the house of Israel" (D&C 39:11; 3 Nephi 16:11).

9. That the gathering centers, as Lehi's son Jacob said, in scattered Israel being "restored to the true church and fold of God" (2 Nephi 9:2). "If they [meaning the Jews] will repent and hearken unto my words," the Lord said, "and harden not their hearts, I will establish my church among them, and they shall come in unto the covenant and be numbered among this the remnant of Jacob," unto whom is given a land of inheritance (see 3 Nephi 21:22).

10. That the gathering centers in accepting Christ as the Book of Mormon bears witness of him (see 3 Nephi 21:1–11).

These are but illustrations, and the list could go on; the point, however, is that we have an entirely different view of what is and of what must take place than do those who do not have living prophets and modern revelation. It is also significant that the events prophesied in the Book of Mormon and the Doctrine and Covenants conform perfectly with the promises or covenant God made with Abraham, promises that centered in his seed having the priesthood and the gospel of salvation.

Conclusion

If we are to be true to our testimony of the Restoration, we must be true to the scriptures of the Restoration. We must come to know them and learn to measure our doctrines against them. Our faith must embrace all that God has revealed, all that he does now reveal, and the assurance that he will yet reveal many great and important things pertaining to the kingdom of God (see Articles of Faith 1:9). All Israel, the ten tribes included, shall yet be gathered to Christ, to the true points of his doctrine, to his Church, and eventually to the lands of their inheritance. The people of the covenant who have wandered far from home shall once again hear the clarion call of their Shepherd as sounded by the mouths of his disciples. And Jehovah's chosen people shall once again find pasture in his fold.

9

The Place of the Covenant

> *The most important single thing that any member of this Church does in this life is to marry the right person in the right place by the right authority.*
> —Bruce R. McConkie

"And it shall come to pass in the last days," wrote both Isaiah and Micah, "that the mountain of the Lord's house shall be established in the top of the mountains, and shall be exalted above the hills; and all nations shall flow unto it. And many people shall go and say, Come ye, and let us go up to the mountain of the Lord, to the house of the God of Jacob; and he will teach us of his ways, and we will walk in his paths: for out of Zion shall go forth the law, and the word of the Lord from Jerusalem." (Isaiah 2:2–3; compare Micah 4:1–2.)

That both writers use the same words suggests the possibility that they were quoting from an even earlier source. In any event, the text is of some considerable moment. It is quoted again in the Book of Mormon (see 2 Nephi 12:2–3) and is commented on in modern revelation, wherein the Lord says: "Let them, therefore, who are among the Gentiles flee unto Zion. And let them who be of Judah flee unto Jerusalem, unto the mountains of the Lord's house." (D&C 133:12–13.) But why all this concern on the part of prophets, ancient and modern, about the Lord's people gathering to a particular place, especially when the promise has been given that the gospel is to be taken to those of every nation, kindred, tongue, and people?

Sacral Space

The truth of God, Joseph Smith said, "will go forth boldly, nobly, and independent, till it has penetrated every continent, visited every clime, swept every country, and sounded in every ear, till the purposes of God shall be accomplished, and the Great Jehovah shall say the work is done" (*History of the Church* 4:540). Such is the destiny of the gospel, the message of salvation; it is to go to all peoples, if not in this life then surely in the next. God has so promised. As Latter-day Saints, we could neither worship nor pay homage to a god who had neither the intent nor the ability to see that all of his children, regardless of the circumstances under which they lived, were granted the privilege of accepting or rejecting the gospel of salvation. In such a belief we stand alone.

It is at great sacrifice, both personal and institutional, that the message of salvation goes forth to fulfill the promise that "the voice of warning shall be unto all people, by the mouths of my disciples, whom I have chosen in these last days" (D&C 1:4). In the imagery of Jeremiah, they go forth as fishers and hunters searching every mountain, hill, and hole in the rocks (see Jeremiah 16:16). In the language of Daniel, the message will be as a stone cut out of the mountain without hands which shall roll forth to fill the whole earth (see Daniel 2:45; D&C 65:2). Isaiah, in a passage quoted anew by many prophets, put it thus: "The ends of the earth shall see the salvation [victory] of our God" (Isaiah 52:10), or as the Lord said to Joseph Smith, "The ends of the earth shall inquire after thy name" (D&C 122:1), meaning, among other things, that people around the world will seek after the blessings of the restored gospel. The promise is sure. The message of salvation will go to all.

Why then the necessity of gathering? Why then the announcement of the ancient prophets that Israel, the children of Jacob, must assume the burden of pain and travail associated with the immigration to the "mountain of the Lord's house" to be instructed, when we have the sure promise that the gospel message will be brought to them?

The answer, though lost to modern Christianity, is simple and can be stated in a single word—*covenants*. The Lord's people have always been a covenant-making people, and thus they have always been a temple-building people, because the temple is the place of the covenant. True it is that the message will go forth, but the message standing independent is not sufficient to save. One cannot say, "Amen, I believe," and thereby satisfy the requirements of heaven. Salvation grows out of the covenant, while Christ, our Savior and Redeemer, is referred to as the "messenger of the covenant" who is to suddenly appear at his temple as part of the great winding-up scene (Malachi 3:1).

Implicit in the ancient prophecy is the verity that some truths are so hallowed and some covenants so sacred that they must be taught or entered into on sacral space, i.e., holy ground. That ground figuratively referred to as "the mountain of the Lord's house" is his temple. Here the covenants we make are made in God's presence, for it is his house, and, as we would assume, before angels and witnesses specially chosen. Here sacred ordinances can be performed that bind the living and the dead. Here time and eternity meet, heaven and earth become one, thus making plain the imagery of the "mountain of the Lord's house." Mountains are nature's temples. They reach to the heavens and give us a clearer view of the eternities. In the rites of the temple, we make a ritual ascent up the mountain as we, like Moses, prepare to pass through the cloud or veil into the divine presence.

Again, true it is that the message of salvation must go to all the world, but that message embraces the instruction for those who accept it to gather, to come to the Lord's house, to stand on sacred ground, and to enjoy that which is too precious to shout from the housetops. A future day will see houses of the Lord, each of them a symbolic mountain, dot the earth, thus making the sacred blessings found therein more readily accessible to all who will receive them.

The Nature and Purpose of Sacral Space

In its origin, the word *sacrifice* meant to make sacred or holy. It comes from the Latin "sacer," meaning "holy," joined with "facere," which means "to make." Since that which is made holy was given to the gods, the word came to mean "to give up." Thus the place of sacrifice was made holy by its very purpose. Anciently, when the Lord's people offered animal sacrifices, they did so on altars. Thus the altar became both the place of sacrifice and the place of covenant-making or covenant renewal. Though altars were built in a variety of locations, they were always to be found in temples, where they were associated with the divine presence. The altar was built on raised ground so that there was a ritual ascent as one approached the place of worship.

Latter-day Saints are the only people of whom we are aware that require it as an article of faith that their people be married in a particular place. Elder Bruce R. McConkie often said, "The most important single thing any member of this Church does in this life is to marry the right person *in the right place* by the right authority." That place is the house of the Lord. Our reverence for place and position is further enhanced as a man and a woman kneel in the Lord's house, facing each other across an altar, to be sealed as husband and wife. Consider the symbolism that is present. The temple, and more particularly the altar, is the place of covenant, the place of the divine presence, and also the place of sacrifice.

What more perfect sermon could be preached to newlyweds than that theirs is a sacred and holy union, one requiring a ritual assent by those clothed in robes symbolic of righteousness and purity, to be bound together by the authority of the priesthood? This ceremony is sanctioned by the presence of God, angels, witnesses, family, and other loved ones, and made sacred by sacrifice. Thus marriage becomes a covenant—a covenant of salvation, a partnership with God, a union to be kept holy, a sacrament that is sanctified by the sacrifice of the man and the woman as they are bound together for time and eternity in a covenant with the Lord and each other.

Thus it was that Adam and Eve became husband and wife in the crowning event of the creation story. The place was Eden, "the garden of God," or "the holy mountain of God" (Ezekiel 28:13–14), while the officiator was he whose garden or mountain it was. There God commanded Adam and Eve to leave father and mother and cleave unto each other and none else (see Moses 3:24). There, in that sanctified state in which death and separation were not known, God "blessed them, and called their name Adam," and commanded that they be one flesh (Genesis 5:2; Moses 6:9). Such is the divine pattern in the house of the Lord, where every man becomes as Adam and every woman becomes as mother Eve, where God makes anew with each man the promises made with father Abraham and with each woman the covenant made with our faithful mother Sarah. Theirs is the promise of endless seed (see D&C 131:1–4; 132:28).

It has ever been so—sacred events require a sacred place, and sacred events make a place sacred. We speak of the land of the prophets as the Holy Land, of the temple as the holy place, and of its most sacred place as the Holy of Holies. Thus we find Enoch recording: "As I was journeying, and stood upon the place Mahujah, and cried unto the Lord, there came a voice out of heaven, saying—Turn ye, and get ye upon the mount Simeon. And it came to pass that I turned and went up on the mount; and as I stood upon the mount, I beheld the heavens open, and I was clothed upon with glory; and I saw the Lord; and he stood before my face, and he talked with me, even as a man talketh one with another, face to face." (Moses 7:2–4.) What made Mount Simeon acceptable to the presence of the Lord while Mahujah was not? We are not told. Presumably, one place was sacred while the other was not.

When God commanded Abraham to sacrifice Isaac, the place of the sacrifice was also specified. It was not enough that he be taken to some convenient hill, but rather the command was that he be taken to "the land of Moriah" and be offered on "one of the mountains" that the Lord would designate. This required a three-day journey on the part of the aged patriarch and his son (see Genesis 22:3–5). The story assumes that the mount was familiar to Abraham and that it already had a religious tradition attached to it. He neither asks for nor is given directions to it. The name is variously defined as meaning "Jehovah provides" or "the Lord shall be manifest" or shall be "seen." Tradition has it that at this same place, in a future day, David would offer a sacrifice, and Jehovah would appear to him. Here it was that the nation of Israel would yet build her temple, and here the sacrificial offerings that typified Christ's atoning sacrifice would be made. Not far from this very spot, the Son of Man would himself be hung on a cross between two thieves.

We see a similar thing in the epic story of Moses and his confrontation with the Pharaoh of Egypt. The Lord wanted to gather his people for the purpose of worship, and only Sinai would do. Why it was necessary that they leave Egypt and make the arduous journey into the wilderness to such a stark and forbidden mountain as Horeb, we are never told in the scriptural account. The place of worship, not the right to worship, was the issue. Moses' appeal to Pharaoh was not for Sabbath closing or freedom of worship. The issue was one of place. The watch cry was, "Let my people go."

Sinai was holy ground. It is referred to in scriptural writ as a holy mount even before Moses stood before the burning bush. Its division into three parts—the boundary at its base beyond which the people could not pass, the side of the mount where the seventy partook of a sacramental meal with their God, and the cloud at the top through which Moses passed to stand in the divine presence—became the pattern for the tabernacle in the wilderness, with its outer court, the holy place, and the Holy of Holies, which in turn was later the pattern for the temple. The temples of the Bible and the world of the Book of Mormon were simply the architectural embodiment of the Sinai experience. The point here is that Sinai was not the place that any of us would have chosen for a family reunion or a weekend away. It is naturally forbidding, not inviting. Those who have been there have suggested that the miracle may not have been the burning bush, but merely the existence of a bush! It was a place apart from the world where the Lord could purify his people and where he could speak to them beyond the range of the unsanctified ear and the gaze of the unhallowed eye. It was the place he had chosen.

Along with Eden, Moriah, and Sinai, mention ought be made of Bethel, which literally means "the house of God." As Jacob was traveling from his father's house at Beersheba to seek a wife in Haran, the Lord appeared to him by night in a marvelous dream. Jacob arose early the next morning and took the stone that had been his pillow and "set it up for a pillar, and poured oil upon the top of it. And he called the name of that place Beth-el: but the name of that city was called Luz at the first." (Genesis 28:10–22.) Years later, upon Jacob's return, God appeared unto him again at the same place, and once more we read that "Jacob set up a pillar in the place where he talked with him, even a pillar of stone: and he poured a drink offering thereon, and he poured oil thereon. And Jacob called the name of the place where God spake with him, Beth-el." (Genesis 35:14–15.) Yet, if we accept the precise definition of the scriptural account, the name *Bethel* existed at this spot even before the arrival of Abram in Canaan (see Genesis 12:8). In future times it would be to this same spot that

Israel would come in times of distress to ask counsel of the Lord (see Judges 20:18, 26, 31; 21:19–20).

The idea of a chosen place was still very much a part of the religious traditions in New Testament times, as evidenced by the Savior's conversation with the Samaritan woman at Jacob's well. "Our fathers worshipped in this mountain," she said, having reference to Mount Gerizim, "and ye say, that in Jerusalem is the place where men ought to worship" (John 4:20). Not only did the mortal Messiah honor his nation's temple traditions, but the resurrected Christ also made his New World appearances at the temple in the land Bountiful (3 Nephi 11:1). It was in one of the great prophecies about the latter days that Malachi announced that the Lord would "suddenly come to his temple" (Malachi 3:1).

Lands of Promise

Nowhere has the prophecy of wars and rumors of wars in the last days seen a more literal fulfillment than in that section of the globe known to us as the Near East. Arab and Jew contend, often with weapons, over a land once known as holy. Each claims a birthright to the land, yet neither seems to understand to whom it has rightfully been promised. In the struggle for possession, both have long since lost the understanding that there are no lands of promise unless that promise also represents the fulfilling of a covenant.

Abraham testified that the Lord appeared to him, saying: "Arise, and take Lot with thee; for I have purposed to take thee away out of Haran, and to make of thee a minister to bear my name in a strange land which I will give unto thy seed after thee for an everlasting possession, *when they hearken to my voice*" (Abraham 2:6, emphasis added). Abraham was to bear the name of the Lord among the inhabitants of what we know as ancient Palestine. He was to be a missionary, declaring the truths of salvation—the principles of faith, repentance, baptism, and the receipt of the Holy Ghost. For valiantly carrying that message, Abraham was promised that he and his posterity would be given that land as an eternal inheritance. Thus it is that the seed of Abraham have claim upon that ancient land as soon as and as long as they hearken unto the Lord's voice, that is, as long as they are a covenant people, a people who bear the name of the Lord, as did their ancient father, and faithfully declare the message of salvation among all the children of men.

Salvation is not associated with *where* we live so much as *how* we live. Possession of a particular plot of ground has never saved a soul. A land of promise is a token of a covenant. It is a tangible reminder of eternal possessions that will be granted those who are true and faithful in the keeping of all gospel covenants. When a given people are true to their covenants, the Lord in turn gives them an earthly possession as a symbol and reminder of the heavenly rewards that will be theirs. When they break those covenants, they lose all rights to the promises of heaven, be these the possession of lands or a place in the eternal realms. Anciently Israel was "gathered" to the lands of their inheritance, where they were expected to be true to their God, honor their covenants, and live in peace. The breaking of those covenants inevitably resulted in their being scattered.

The Savior's prophecy to the Jews of the destruction of their temple was most ominous. The temple, as we have noted, is the place of the covenant, and as long as the temple stood it symbolized to that people that the hand of the Lord was over them. To prophesy its destruction was tantamount to prophesying their destruction as a nation. To further prophesy that not one stone of the sacred edifice would be left standing on another was to prophesy that her people would be scattered among all the nations of the earth, which is, indeed what has happened. Thus, perhaps the greatest prophecy of the last days centers in the building anew of that temple, for it will symbolize the true gathering of Israel, a gathering not to a political kingdom but rather to the Lord and his principles of salvation. It will represent Israel's acceptance once again of the terms and conditions of the ancient covenant that God made with their fathers. With it will come the token of that covenant, i.e., a land of promise, a land of peace and prosperity, for once again the protecting hand of the Lord will be over his people, a people who have taken upon them his name.

In commenting on the prophecies of Isaiah, Nephi assured his readers that "the Lord God will proceed" in the last days "to make bare his arm in the eyes of all the nations, in bringing about his covenants and his gospel unto those who are of the house of Israel. Wherefore, he will bring them again out of captivity, and they shall be gathered together to the lands of their inheritance; and they shall be brought out of obscurity and out of darkness; and they shall know that the Lord is their Savior and their Redeemer, the Mighty One of Israel." (1 Nephi 22:11–12.) Jacob, brother of Nephi, declared that the Lord had "covenanted with all the house of Israel" that when that day came in which they returned to "the true church and fold of God" they would again be "gathered home to the lands of their inheritance" and be "established in all their lands of promise" (2 Nephi 9:1–2).

The Book of Mormon, the scriptural record destined to come forth in the last days for the purpose of actuating the gathering of Israel, is both plain and emphatic in the declaration that the tribes of Israel have claim to "lands" of promise when they once again accept "the fulness" of the gospel and believe in Jesus Christ as the Son of God. "Then will the Father gather them together again, and give unto them Jerusalem for a land of their inheritance" (3 Nephi 20:33).

Conclusion

The temple is a house of revelation. It is the place of covenant. It is the place where the God of Abraham, Isaac, and Jacob continues to reveal himself to his chosen people. The temple is also the place where every faithful member of the Church may, both figuratively and literally, stand in the presence of the divine. It is there that the God of Jacob teaches his covenant children of his ways and how they may walk in his paths (see Isaiah 2:2–3). It is the place where his appointed servants gather regularly to wait upon him and to obtain his will concerning his earthly kingdom. The temple is more than a monument to faith. It is a source of faith. It is an unspoken sermon of unmatched eloquence. It is a building with a message.

10

Millennial Israel: One Fold and One Shepherd

And the time cometh speedily that the righteous must be led up as calves of the stall, and the Holy One of Israel must reign in dominion, and might, and power, and great glory.
—1 Nephi 22:24

The call and preparation of the house of Israel—a labor that began before the foundations of the earth were laid and continues in this the second estate—shall come to consummation in the Millennium. The Father's work and his tender regard and care for his chosen people shall go on during the thousand years of peace. Israel shall be gathered, organized, and put in place, all in preparation for the time when they shall rule and reign in celestial glory in the kingdoms and worlds to come.

Unto All Nations

Both the Old Testament and the Book of Mormon attest that a significant part of the drama we know as the gathering of Israel will be millennial, that is, it will be brought to pass after the second coming of Jesus Christ in glory. Between now and then we shall see marvelous things on the earth in regard to the people of Israel coming to their Lord and King and thereafter to the lands of their inheritance.

We have witnessed already the phenomenal gathering of many thousands of the seed of Lehi (of the tribe of Joseph) into the Church, and this is but the beginning. We have stood in awe as Jacob's descendants around the globe have been found, identified, taught, and converted to the faith of their fathers, and yet we have seen but the tip of the iceberg. We would expect that soon our missionaries will enter into lands wherein pockets of Israelites will be baptized and confirmed and where patriarchs will declare their lineage through such tribes as Issachar, Zebulun, Gad, Asher, and Naphtali.

The Savior himself foretold that "this Gospel of the Kingdom shall be preached in all the world, for a witness unto all nations, and then shall the end come, or the destruction of the wicked" (Joseph Smith—Matthew 1:31). It is not sufficient, however, for the message of the Restoration to be delivered to every nation. John the Revelator spoke of another matter—the fact that before the Lord's coming in glory, there would be kings and priests in every nation, kindred, tongue, and people (see Revelation 5:9–10), meaning that the fulness of the blessings of the house of the Lord would also be available to those peoples. Elder Bruce R. McConkie prophesied in 1980:

> Looking ahead we see the gospel preached in all nations and to every people with success attending. We see the Lord break down the barriers so that the world of Islam and the world of Communism can hear the message of the restoration; and we glory in the fact that Ishmael—as well as Isaac—and Esau—as well as Jacob—shall have an inheritance in the eternal kingdom.
>
> We see congregations of the covenant people worshipping the Lord in Moscow and Peking and Saigon. We see Saints of the Most High raising their voices in Egypt and India and Africa.
>
> We see stakes of Zion in all parts of the earth; and Israel, the chosen people, gathering into these cities of holiness, as it were, to await the coming of their King.
>
> We see temples in great numbers dotting the earth, so that those of every nation and kindred and tongue and people can receive the fulness of the ordinances of the house of the Lord and can qualify to live and reign as kings and priests on earth a thousand years. (Conference Report, April 1980, pp. 98–99.)

As we have noted earlier, a major conversion of the Jews will take place near the time of the Lord's coming in glory. "And it shall come to pass in that day," Jehovah said through Zechariah, "that I will seek to destroy all the nations that come against Jerusalem. And I will pour upon the house of David, and upon the inhabitants of Jerusalem, the spirit of grace and of supplications: and they shall look upon me whom they have pierced, and they shall mourn for him, as one mourneth for his only son, and shall be in bitterness for him, as one that is in bitterness for his firstborn. . . . And one shall say unto him, What are these wounds in thine hands? Then he shall answer, Those with which I was wounded in the house of my friends." (Zechariah 12:9–10; 13:6.)

A modern revelation describes in greater detail this poignant moment in our Lord's dealings with his own. After he has set his foot on the Mount of Olives and the mountain has cleaved in twain, "Then shall the Jews look upon me and say: What are these wounds in thine hands and in thy feet? Then shall they know that I am the Lord; for I will say unto them: These wounds are the wounds with which I was wounded in the house of my friends. I am he who was lifted up. I am Jesus that was crucified. I am the Son of God. And then shall they weep because of their iniquities; then shall they lament because they persecuted their king." (D&C 45:48–53.) Before this time Jews from around the globe will already have investigated the message of the Restoration, entered into the covenant gospel, and come home to the God of Abraham, Isaac, and Jacob. They will not only have come to acknowledge Jesus as an honorable prophet-teacher but will also confess him as Lord and God, the promised Messiah. Their garments will have been "washed in the blood of the Lamb" (Ether 13:11), meaning that they will have been cleansed and renewed through the ordinances and the workings of the Holy Spirit. But at the time the Master appears at Olivet, the conversion of a nation will begin.

The Work of the Father Commences

As he began to close his first book, and as a part of his commentary on Isaiah 49, Nephi wrote of the fate of all persons or organizations in the last days that fight against the Church and Kingdom of the Lamb. They shall be destroyed, he pointed out, as will that great and abominable church that is the whore of all the earth. "For behold, saith the prophet"—presumably Zenos—"the time cometh speedily that Satan shall have no more power over the hearts of the children of men; for the day soon cometh that all the proud and they who do wickedly shall be as stubble; and the day cometh that they must be burned. For the time soon cometh that the fulness of the wrath of God shall be poured out upon all the children of men; for he will not suffer that the wicked shall destroy the righteous." The day is near at hand when the Lord Jesus shall return with a glory that shall be to the wicked as a devouring fire. Indeed, the great and dreadful day of the Lord shall be a selective burning, a fire that consumes the wicked but spares and sanctifies the faithful. Thus Nephi added: "He will preserve the righteous by his power, even if it so be that the fulness of his wrath must come, and the righteous be preserved, even unto the destruction of their enemies by fire. Wherefore, the righteous need not fear; for thus saith the prophet, they shall be saved, even if it so be as by fire." (1 Nephi 22:14–17.)

Nephi's oracle continues. Those who perpetuate priestcraft and all "those who seek the lusts of the flesh and the things of the world . . . are they who need fear, and tremble, and quake." Nephi then speaks of a time of gathering, a day "that the righteous must be led up as calves of the stall, and the Holy One of Israel must reign in dominion, and might, and power, and great glory." It is the day of millennial glory. Christ the Lord dwells with his people. In that day—a time when the wicked have been removed from the newly-cleansed terrestrial earth, when an era of righteousness has been brought in by power but is maintained by the righteousness of the people—the work of the Father commences anew: "And [Christ the Lord] gathereth his children from the four quarters of the earth; and he numbereth his sheep, and they know him; and there shall be one fold and one shepherd; and he shall feed his sheep, and in him they shall find pasture." (1 Nephi 22:23–26; compare 2 Nephi 30:6–18.)

In speaking in person to his Nephite disciples, Jesus described that millennial day when all the enemies of Israel would be cut off. "And I will gather my people together as a man gathereth his sheaves into the floor" (3 Nephi 20:18). He further explained that the Gentiles—meaning, in this case, those legal administrators in The Church of Jesus Christ of Latter-day Saints authorized to offer the blessings of the gospel and the priesthood to the lost sheep of the house of Israel (see Joseph Fielding Smith, *Doctrines of Salvation* 2:246–51; Spencer W. Kimball, *Teachings of Spencer W. Kimball*, pp. 600–601)—"shall . . .

assist my people that they may be gathered in, who are scattered upon all the face of the land, in unto the New Jerusalem. And then shall the power of heaven come down among them; and I also will be in the midst." And now note this most unusual statement: "And then shall the work of the Father commence at that day, even when this gospel shall be preached among the remnant of this people." (3 Nephi 21:24–26.)

Then shall the work commence? *Commence?* The work of the gathering of Israel commenced in earnest even before the Church was organized. The work of gathering was formalized in 1836 with the coming of Moses to the Kirtland Temple to deliver the keys of the gathering of Israel. Why, then, would the Lord speak of commencing his work in the Millennium?

Simply stated, the magnitude and magnificence and breadth and depth of the gathering in that glorious day will be such as to cause all previous efforts at gathering to pale into insignificance. It will be as though the work had just begun. In speaking specifically of the millennial gathering, the Savior then spoke of the lost tribes: "Verily I say unto you, at that day shall the work of the Father commence among all the dispersed of my people, yea, even the tribes which have been lost, which the Father hath led away out of Jerusalem. Yea, the work shall commence among all the dispersed of my people, with the Father to prepare the way whereby they may come unto me, that they may call on the Father in my name. Yea, and then shall the work commence, with the Father among all nations in preparing the way whereby his people may be gathered home to the land of their inheritance." (3 Nephi 21:26–28.)

When the Lord comes in his glory, those who are of a telestial nature will be removed from the earth and sent to the postmortal spirit world to await the last resurrection. Those who remain will be of either a celestial or a terrestrial nature, the latter category consisting of the "honorable men of the earth" who receive the testimony that Jesus is the Christ but are not valiant enough in their faith to receive Christ's covenant gospel and join his true Church; also those who hold Church membership but are "not valiant" (see D&C 76:74–75, 79). The Prophet Joseph Smith, presumably speaking of terrestrial persons, said: "There will be wicked men on the earth during the thousand years. The heathen nations who will not come up to worship will be visited with the judgments of God, and must eventually be destroyed from the earth." (*Teachings*, pp. 268–69.) Thus, as Elder Bruce R. McConkie observed,

> there will be many churches on earth when the Millennium begins. False worship will continue among those whose desires are good, "who are honorable men of the earth," but who have been "blinded by the craftiness of men." (D&C 76:75.) Plagues will rest upon them until they repent and believe the gospel or are destroyed, as the Prophet said. It follows that missionary work will continue into the Millennium until all who remain are converted. Then "the earth shall be full of the knowledge of the Lord, as the waters cover the sea." (Isaiah 11:9.) Then every living soul on earth will belong to The Church of Jesus Christ of Latter-day Saints. (*The Millennial Messiah*, p. 652; see also Joseph Fielding Smith, *Doctrines of Salvation* 1:86–87.)

In that glorious era of peace and goodness, the dispersed of Israel shall receive the message of the Restoration, read and believe the Book of Mormon, traverse the "highway of righteousness" (see Isaiah 35:8) into the true Church, and take their place beside their kinsmen in the household of faith. The revelations declare that "their enemies shall become a prey unto them" (D&C 133:28). That is, the enemies of Israel—the wicked and carnal elements of a fallen world—will have been destroyed by the glory and power of the Second Coming. There will have been "an entire separation of the righteous and the wicked"; the enemies of the chosen people will be no more, because the Lord will have sent forth his angels "to pluck out the wicked and cast them into unquenchable fire" (D&C 63:54). Truly, "such of the gathering of Israel as has come to pass so far is but the gleam of a star that soon will be hidden by the splendor of the sun in full blaze; truly, the magnitude and grandeur and glory of the gathering is yet to be" (Bruce R. McConkie, *The Millennial Messiah*, p. 196).

The Second David Reigns

The Prophet Joseph Smith taught: "Although David was a king, he never did obtain the spirit and power of Elijah and the fullness of the Priesthood; and the Priesthood that he received, and the throne and kingdom of David is to be taken from him and given to another by the name of David in the last days, raised up out of his lineage" (*Teachings*,

p. 339). So far as we can tell, the modern seer never offered prophetic commentary or further explanation on this statement. The scriptures, however, provide our best source of understanding on this subject.

David the king was adored by his people. He united the kingdom, thwarted and defeated the enemies of Israel, and stood as a shining illustration of God's love for his chosen. Though David, through sin, fell from his high standing and lost his exaltation (see D&C 132:39), he remained in the minds and hearts of Israelites through the ages as the prototype of Israel's king. Jesus came to earth as a descendant of David and as a perfect fulfillment of the prophetic promise given to the son of Jesse: "Thine house and thy kingdom shall be established for ever before thee: thy throne shall be established for ever" (2 Samuel 7:16). Indeed, "mighty David became the similitude for the very Messiah himself. As David slew Goliath and saved Israel from the Philistines, so the Messiah would break the Gentile bands and remove from his people the alien yoke. As David united and ruled over the Twelve Tribes of Israel, so the Messiah would unite the two kingdoms, Judah and Israel, and reign over one people in peace and glory forever." (Bruce R. McConkie, *The Millennial Messiah*, p. 602.) Jesus was the son of David. And in a future day, the Millennium, this son of David, the second David—the Millennial Messiah himself—shall rule and reign over his people.

The Lord spoke through Jeremiah: "Behold, the days come, saith the Lord, that I will raise unto David a righteous Branch, and a King shall reign and prosper, and shall execute judgment and justice in the earth. In his days Judah shall be saved, and Israel shall dwell safely: and this is his name whereby he shall be called, THE LORD OUR RIGHTEOUSNESS" (Jeremiah 23:5–6; compare 33:15–22). Further: "It shall come to pass in that day, saith the Lord of hosts, that I will break his yoke from off thy neck, and will burst thy bonds, and strangers shall no more serve themselves of him: but they shall serve the Lord their God, and David their king, whom I will raise up unto them" (Jeremiah 30:8–9). This David will be the King and Prince of Israel (see Ezekiel 37:24–25). "For the children of Israel shall abide many days without a king, and without a prince, and without a sacrifice, and without an image, and without an ephod, and without teraphim: afterward shall the children of Israel return, and seek the Lord their God, and David their king; and shall fear the Lord and his goodness in the latter days" (Hosea 3:4–5).

The Psalmist certified that "The Lord"—meaning Jehovah, who is Jesus Christ—"is my shepherd" (Psalm 23:1), and Jesus of Nazareth himself declared in the meridian of time: "I am the good shepherd" (John 10:14). How appropriate, therefore, that our Master should refer to himself as David the Shepherd. "Therefore will I save my flock, and they shall no more be a prey. . . . And I will set up one shepherd over them, and he shall feed them, even my servant David; he shall feed them, and he shall be their shepherd. And I the Lord will be their God, and my servant David a prince among them; I the Lord have spoken it." (Ezekiel 34:22–24.)

The Latter-day Saints need not be deceived on this matter. We need not look for one mighty and strong, for a special servant who shall in some way gain kingly authority. "This wresting of the written word," Elder McConkie has written, "assumes that someone of prophetic stature will arise in the Church in the last days, to preside as a Second David, and to prepare the way before the Second Coming of the Son of Man. That there may be one or many brethren called David who preside over the Church in this dispensation is of no moment. The scriptures that speak of King David reigning in the last days are Messianic; they have reference to the Millennial reign of the Lord Jesus Christ." (*New Witness*, p. 518; see also *The Millennial Messiah*, pp. 589–611.) The divine word to the members of the Church is sure: "Be subject to the powers that be, *until he reigns whose right it is to reign*, and subdues all enemies under his feet" (D&C 58:22, emphasis added). In the words of Elder John Taylor, in the Millennium the kingdom of God will be established "on a literal earth, and will be composed of literal men, women, and children; of living saints who keep the commandments of God, and of resurrected bodies who shall actually come out of their graves, and live on the earth. The Lord will be king over all the earth, and all mankind literally under his sovereignty, and every nation under the heavens will have to acknowledge his authority, and bow to his sceptre. . . . This may properly be called the day of reckoning, . . . when the rightful heir shall possess the kingdom." (*The Government of God*, pp. 87–88.)

Neither Jew nor Greek

One of the most graphic prophetic statements about Israel in the

Millennium is contained in the writings of Zenos, one of the prophets on the brass plates. In speaking of what appears to be the millennial day, Zenos taught:

> And there began to be the natural fruit again in the vineyard; and the natural branches began to grow and thrive exceedingly; and the wild branches began to be plucked off and to be cast away; and they did keep the root and the top thereof equal, according to the strength thereof.
> And thus they labored, with all diligence, according to the commandments of the Lord of the vineyard, even until the bad had been cast away out of the vineyard, and the Lord had preserved unto himself that the trees had become again the natural fruit; and they became like unto one body; and the fruits were equal; and the Lord of the vineyard had preserved unto himself the natural fruit, which was most precious unto him from the beginning. (Jacob 5:73–74.)

The feuding and the dissensions between Israel and Judah will be no more. The fighting and the quarreling over land and water and rights will come to an end. "The envy of Ephraim also shall depart, and the adversaries of Judah shall be cut off; Ephraim shall not envy Judah, and Judah shall not vex Ephraim" (2 Nephi 21:13). In that supernal day, the promise of God to his chosen people will be well on the way to fulfillment.

Paul's words, spoken in the meridian of time, will then have particular relevance. "As many of you as have been baptized into Christ," he observed, "have put on Christ. There is neither Jew nor Greek, there is neither bond nor free, there is neither male nor female: for ye are all one in Christ Jesus. And if ye be Christ's, then are ye Abraham's seed, and heirs according to the promise." (Galatians 3:27–29.) All those who come unto Christ, who is the Holy One of Israel, shall, under Christ, rule and reign in the house of Israel forever. In the millennial day the Lord Jehovah will reign personally upon the earth (see Articles of Faith 1:10). More specifically, "Christ and the resurrected Saints will reign over the earth during the thousand years. They will not probably dwell upon the earth [permanently], but will visit it when they please, or when it is necessary to govern it." (*Teachings*, p. 268.) In that day he shall preside as King of kings and Lord of lords: Israel's Good Shepherd shall be in the midst of his chosen people and minister to them in everlasting splendor.

Conclusion

The blossoming and ultimate fulfillment of the Abrahamic covenant, the new and everlasting covenant restored through Joseph Smith, will be millennial. The principles and ordinances of the gospel, the articles of adoption by which men and women are received into the royal family and given a rightful place in the house of Israel, will continue to be taught and observed during the thousand years. A modern apostle has written:

> During the Millennium children will be named and blessed by the elders of the kingdom. When those of the rising generation arrive at the years of accountability, they will be baptized in water and of the Spirit by legal administrators appointed so to act. Priesthood will be conferred upon young and old, and they will be ordained to offices therein as the needs of the ministry and their own salvation require. At the appropriate time each person will receive his patriarchal blessing, we suppose from the natural patriarch who presides in his family, as it was in Adamic days and as it was when Jacob blessed his sons. The saints will receive their endowments in the temples of the Lord, and they will receive the blessings of celestial marriage at their holy altars. And all the faithful will have their callings and elections made sure and will be sealed up unto that eternal life which will come to them when they reach the age of a tree. (Bruce R. McConkie, *The Millennial Messiah*, pp. 673–74.)

"Behold," Jeremiah wrote, "the days come, saith the Lord, that I will make a new covenant with the house of Israel, and with the house of Judah: not according to the covenant that I made with their fathers in the day that I took them by the hand to bring them out of the land of Egypt; . . . but this shall be the covenant that I will make with the house of Israel; After those days, saith the Lord, I will put my law in their inward parts, and write it in their hearts; and will be their God, and they shall be my people." What a glorious and remarkable day that will be, a time when the law of the Lord is emblazoned on the souls of those who walk the earth! The word continues: "And they shall teach no more every man his neighbour, and every man his brother, saying, Know the Lord: for they shall all know me, from the least of them unto the greatest of them, saith the Lord: for I will forgive their iniquity, and I will remember their sin no more." (Jeremiah 31:31–34.)

That is to say, in a day soon to break upon this world, there shall be a people who know their God and are disposed to keep his commandments. They will walk and talk with him, and, we presume, with other holy beings. It will be the day of Israel's glory, the day when the Holy One reigns among the people of covenant. In that day when men and women are filled with the knowledge of the Lord, "and shall see eye to eye," they will "lift up their voice, and with the voice together sing this new song, saying:

> The Lord hath brought again Zion;
> The Lord hath redeemed his people, Israel,
> According to the election of grace,
> Which was brought to pass by the faith
> And covenant of their fathers.
>
> The Lord hath redeemed his people;
> And Satan is bound and time is no longer.
> The Lord hath gathered all things in one.
> The Lord hath brought down Zion from above.
> The Lord hath brought up Zion from beneath.
>
> The earth hath travailed and brought forth her strength;
> And truth is established in her bowels;
> And the heavens have smiled upon her;
> And she is clothed with the glory of her God;
> For he stands in the midst of his people.
>
> Glory, and honor, and power, and might,
> Be ascribed to our God; for he is full of mercy,
> Justice, grace and truth, and peace,
> Forever and ever, Amen. (D&C 84:98–102.)

Epilogue

"When the Lord shall come," a modern revelation explains, "he shall reveal all things—things which have passed, and hidden things which no man knew, things of the earth, by which it was made, and the purpose and the end thereof—things most precious, things that are above, and things that are beneath, things that are in the earth, and upon the earth, and in heaven" (D&C 101:32–34). When the Lion of the tribe of Judah finally unseals the scrolls that contain "the revealed will, mysteries, and the works of God," even "the hidden things of his economy concerning this earth during the seven thousand years of its continuance, or its temporal existence" (D&C 77:6; see also Revelation 5:1), then surely we shall one and all come to know of his peculiar dealings with Israel, of the strange but masterful manner in which he has moved upon and through his covenant people in mysterious ways his wonders to perform.

In 1882 Elder Erastus Snow delivered one of the most penetrating discourses on the role and mission of Israel in all our literature. In speaking of those who come to the earth as descendants of Abraham in the last days, he said:

> The Lord has sent those noble spirits into the world to perform a special work, and appointed their times; and they have always fulfilled the mission given them, and their future glory and exaltation is secured unto them; and that is what I understand by the doctrine of election spoken of by the Apostle Paul and other sacred writers. . . . Such were called and chosen and elected of God to perform a certain work at a certain time in the world's history and in due time he fitted them for that work. . . .

Their blood has permeated European society, and it coursed in the veins of the early colonists in America. And when the books shall be opened and the lineage of all men is known, it will be found that they have been first and foremost in everything noble among men in the various nations in breaking off the shackles of kingcraft and priestcraft and oppression of every kind, and the foremost among men in upholding and maintaining the principles of liberty and freedom upon this continent and establishing a representative government, and thus preparing the way for the coming forth of the fulness of the everlasting Gospel. And it is the foremost of those spirits whom the Lord has prepared to receive the Gospel when it was presented to them, and who did not wait for the Elders to hunt them from the hills and corners of the earth, but they were hunting for the Elders, impelled by a spirit which then they could not understand; and for this reason were they among the first Elders of the Church; they and the fathers having been watched over from the days that God promised those blessings upon Isaac and Jacob and Joseph and Ephraim. And these are they that will be found in the front ranks of all that is noble and good in their day and time, and who will be found among those whose efforts are directed in establishing upon the earth those heaven-born principles which tend directly to blessing and salvation, to ameliorating the condition of their fellowmen, and elevating them in the scale of their being; and among those also who receive the fullness of the everlasting Gospel, and the keys of Priesthood in the last days, through whom God determined to gather up again unto himself a peculiar people, a holy nation, a pure seed that shall stand upon Mount Zion as saviors. (JD 23:185–87.)

And so to those who have come unto Christ through the everlasting covenant, we echo the words of Mormon: "Know ye that ye are of the house of Israel" (Mormon 7:2). Or as Jesus declared: "Ye are the children of the prophets; and ye are of the house of Israel; and ye are of the covenant which the Father made with your fathers, saying unto Abraham: And in thy seed shall all the kindreds of the earth be blessed" (3 Nephi 20:25). "I am reminded," President Harold B. Lee said in his last address to Brigham Young University students, "of the old court jester who was supposed to entertain his king with interesting stories and antics. He looked at the king who was lolling on his throne, a drunken, filthy rascal; [he] doffed his cap and bells, and said with a mock gesture of obeisance, 'O king, be loyal to the royal within you.' " ("Be Loyal to the Royal Within You," *1973 BYU Speeches of the Year*, p. 100.)

We affirm that our patriarchal blessings specify literal blood descent, and—because of our connection to father Abraham and through the call and ministry of a modern Abraham and the keys and powers delivered to him—ours is the right to the gospel, the priesthood, and the glories of eternal life. We need not misunderstand this matter and should not confuse ancestry with adoption; this matter of lineal descent is neither myth nor metaphor. Nor should those who are not directly descended from Israel who join the Church feel in any way less than chosen. Chosenness is a status based upon the choice to follow the Lord and associate with his people, and entrance into the true Church qualifies one for the blessings of Ephraim, as though he or she had been born a child of Abraham.

We further testify that the Lord has set his hand again a second time to gather his people Israel and that the great work of the Restoration entails the gathering of Israel, first to Christ and his gospel and then to the lands of their inheritance. The keys of the gathering of Israel are held in their entirety by the President of The Church of Jesus Christ of Latter-day Saints. That Church is now in the line of its duty, is and will be involved intimately in the gathering of Abraham's descendants into the true fold of God, and in so doing is preparing a people for the return to earth of the King of Zion, who is the Holy One of Israel. The keys of the kingdom of God—the supernal power by which men and women may be endowed, married for eternity, and sealed up unto eternal life—are held and exercised by Apostles and prophets and also by others to whom these rights and privileges are delegated.

Our duty is to walk with fidelity and devotion, to proceed on the strait and narrow path with humility so as to be worthy of the name and lineage that is ours. By so doing we shall help to bring to pass God's foreordained purposes for us and our families. It can then be said of us as it was of Abraham: "I know him, that he will command his children and his household after him, and they shall keep the way of the Lord, to do justice and judgment" (Genesis 18:19). The whole history of the house of Israel attests to the endowment of power and the blessing of protection that come to those who are true to their covenants. Conversely, the sobering reality to be found in that same history is that those who shirk or ignore their promises become the servants of sorrow and wander in the morass of spiritual darkness. They lose their way and forfeit their birthright. The Prophet thus wrote poetically of those who spurn the new and everlasting covenant:

> For they never received the gospel of Christ,
> Nor the prophetic spirit that came from the Lord;
> Nor the covenant neither, which Jacob once had;
> They went their own way, and they have their reward
> (*Times and Seasons* 4:85).

As we remain loyal to our heritage—to who we are, to whose we are, and thus to what we may become—we eventually make our calling and election sure to the promised rewards and secure a place everlastingly with those who preceded us in a similar endeavor. "And may the Lord bless you," Alma pleaded, "and keep your garments spotless, that ye may at last be brought to sit down with Abraham, Isaac, and Jacob, and the holy prophets who have been ever since the world began, having your garments spotless even as their garments are spotless, in the kingdom of heaven to go no more out" (Alma 7:25). Such is our opportunity and our great challenge, our glory or our condemnation.

Bibliography

Anderson, James H. *God's Covenant Race.* Salt Lake City: Deseret News Press, 1938.

Arrington, Leonard J., and Davis Bitton. *The Mormon Experience, A History of the Latter-day Saints.* New York: Alfred A. Knopf, 1979.

Ballard, Melvin J. "The Three Degrees of Glory," in *Melvin J. Ballard—Crusader for Righteousness.* Salt Lake City: Bookcraft, 1966.

Bennett, Archibald F. *Saviors on Mount Zion.* Salt Lake City: Deseret Sunday School Union Board, 1950.

Bible Knowledge Commentary, ed. John F. Walvoord and Roy B. Zuck. Wheaton, Il.: Victor Books, 1985.

Collected Discourses. Woodland Hills, Utah: B. H. S. Publishing, 1988.

Collegeville Bible Commentary, ed. Dianne Beragant and Robert J. Karris. Collegeville, Minn.: Liturgical Press, 1989.

Conference Report. Salt Lake City: The Church of Jesus Christ of Latter-day Saints, April 1967; October 1973; April 1974; April 1980; October 1983; April 1987; October 1992.

Conference Report of the Mexico and Central America Area Conference, August 1972.

Deseret News Weekly. Salt Lake City, August 31, 1854.

Dictionary of Christ and the Gospels, 2 vols., ed. James Hastings. Edinburgh: T&T Clark, 1906.

Ginzberg, Louis. *Legends of the Jews*, 7 vols. Philadelphia: The Jewish Publication Society of America, 1937.

Harper's Bible Dictionary, ed. Paul J. Achtemeier. San Francisco: Harper & Row, 1985.

Hymns of The Church of Jesus Christ of Latter-day Saints. Salt Lake City: Corporation of the President of The Church of Jesus Christ of Latter-day Saints, 1985.

Journal History, 23 February 1847, comp. Andrew Jenson, et al. Salt Lake City: Historical Department of The Church of Jesus Christ of Latter-day Saints, 1906.

Journal of Discourses, 26 vols. Liverpool: F. D. Richards & Sons, 1851–86.

Kimball, Spencer W. "Be Ye Therefore Perfect." Address given at the Institute of Religion at the University of Utah, 10 January 1975.

———. *The Teachings of Spencer W. Kimball,* ed. Edward L. Kimball. Salt Lake City: Bookcraft, 1982.

Lee, Harold B. "Be Loyal to the Royal Within You," in *1973 Brigham Young University Speeches of the Year.* Provo, Utah: Brigham Young University Publications, 1973.

———. "The Place of the Living Prophet, Seer, and Revelator," in Brent L. Top, Larry E. Dahl, Walter D. Bowen, *Follow the Living Prophets.* Salt Lake City: Bookcraft, 1993.

Leon-Dufour, Xavier. *Dictionary of the New Testament.* New York: Harper & Row, 1980.

Little, James A., and Franklin D. Richards. *A Compendium of the Doctrines of the Gospel,* revised. Salt Lake City: Deseret Book Co., 1925.

McCarthy, Dennis J. *Treaty and Covenant.* Rome: Biblical Institute Press, 1978.

McConkie, Bruce R. *The Millennial Messiah.* Salt Lake City: Deseret Book Co., 1982.

———. *The Mortal Messiah,* 4 vols. Salt Lake City: Deseret Book Co., 1979–81.

———. *A New Witness for the Articles of Faith.* Salt Lake City: Deseret Book Co., 1985.

McConkie, Joseph F. *His Name Shall Be Joseph.* Salt Lake City: Hawkes Publishing Inc., 1980.

McConkie, Joseph F., and Robert L. Millet. *Doctrinal Commentary on the Book of Mormon,* 4 vols. Salt Lake City: Bookcraft, 1987–1992.

———, and Robert L. Millet. *The Holy Ghost.* Salt Lake City: Bookcraft, 1989.

Messages of the First Presidency, 6 vols., comp. James R. Clark. Salt Lake City: Bookcraft, 1965–75.

Millennial Star. Liverpool: The Church of Jesus Christ of Latter-day Saints, 1840–1970.

Millet, Robert L., and Joseph F. McConkie. *The Life Beyond.* Salt Lake City: Bookcraft, 1986.

Nelson, Russell M. "Thanks for the Covenant," in *1988–89 Brigham Young University Devotional and Fireside Speeches.* Provo, Utah: Brigham Young University Publications, 1989.

Nicholson, E. W. "The Interpretation of Exodus XXIV 9–11," *Veta Testamentum,* vol. 24, no. 1, January 1974.

Packer, Boyd K. "To Be Learned Is Good If . . ." *Ensign,* November 1992.

Seeking After Our Dead: Our Greatest Responsibility. Salt Lake City: Genealogical Society of Utah, 1928.

Smith, Joseph Fielding. *Doctrines of Salvation,* 3 vols., comp. Bruce R. McConkie. Salt Lake City: Bookcraft, 1954–56.

Smith, Joseph, Jr. *History of The Church of Jesus Christ of Latter-day Saints,* 7 vols., ed. B. H. Roberts. Salt Lake City: The Church of Jesus Christ of Latter-day Saints, 1932–51.

———. *Teachings of the Prophet Joseph Smith.*, comp. Joseph Fielding Smith. Salt Lake City: Deseret Book Co., 1976.

Stevenson, Edward. *Reminiscences of Joseph, the Prophet, and the Coming Forth of the Book of Mormon.* Salt Lake City: Edward Stevenson, 1893.

Taylor, John. *The Government of God.* Liverpool: S. W. Richards, 1852.

Times and Seasons. 6 vols. Nauvoo, Illinois: The Church of Jesus Christ of Latter-day Saints, 1839–46.

Top, Brent L. *The Life Before.* Salt Lake City: Bookcraft, 1988.

Utah Genealogical and Historical Magazine, 31 vols. Salt Lake City: Genealogical Society of Utah, 1910–1940; January 1930, October 1934.

Whitney, Orson F. *Elias: An Epic of the Ages.* New York: The Knickerbocker Press, 1904.

Index

— A —

Abraham, blessings promised to, 8–10, 101–2
  commanded to sacrifice Isaac, 123
  descendants to administer priesthood, 21
  family history, 41–45, 123
  meaning of names, 42
Abrahamic covenant, and restoration of gospel, 31
  description, 41, 42–44
  forsaken by Israel, 66–67
  fulfillment in Millennium, 138
  sealing Church members to, 75
  terms and conditions, 31–32
  See also Gospel covenant
"Abraham's bosom," place of faithful departed spirits, 9
Abraham's seed, 25–26, 48–49, 62, 101–2, 113, 137
  has "believing blood," 19
  to bear priesthood among all nations, 108
  See also Abraham; Abrahamic covenant; House of Israel
Adam, 53
  and patriarchal order, 39–41
Adam and Eve, 1
  enter into covenant with God, 13
  marriage, 36, 122
Agency, 16
  and foreordination, 25
  and keeping commandments, 23
Alma the Younger, on worthiness to join prophets hereafter, 144
  on those who harden hearts and blind minds, 25
Altar, place of divine presence, 122
Apostasy, a cause for scattering, 67
  compared to adultery, 34
  in Abraham's day, 43–44
  in latter days, 13
  of lost ten tribes, 47
  universal, 5
Atonement, 2, 70, 80–81

— B —

Babylon, 47, 70
Ballard, Melvin J., on foreordination of Israel, 17
Baptism, 7
  a means of gathering, 71, 73
  among Nephites, 12, 90
  and Quorum of Twelve, 91–93
  Nephites receive instructions and authority for, 90
  of Christ, 11
  ordinance by which people enter covenant, 91–93
  part of Jews' messianic tradition, 11–12
Bennett, Archibald F., on Church

leaders' ancestry, 54
Benson, Ezra Taft, on Book of Mormon as instrument of gathering, 79
Bethel, 124
Bible, 48, 85, 129
    and Book of Mormon, 79–81
    plain and precious things missing, 5–8, 12, 43
Birthright, 90
    blessings and obligations of, 101–2
    passed to Joseph (son of Jacob), 32, 45
Bondage, deliverance from, 32, 52, 113, 126
    of Israelites in Egypt, 45
    to Rome during Christ's ministry, 47
Book of Mormon, 86–87
    and Bible, 6, 79–81, 85
    instrument for establishing Zion, 81
    on scattering of Israel, 66–69
    purposes of, 31
    vital part of gathering of Israel, 77–82, 99, 101–2, 115, 129
    witness of Jesus Christ, 31, 81–82

— C —

Calling and election, 2, 16, 21
    conditional, 25
    made sure, 60, 144
Cameron, W. J., on special service for chosen people, 22
Cannon, George Q., on being gathered, 80
Chosen people, description, 2–3, 33, 141–42
    See also Covenant people; House of Israel
Church of Jesus Christ of Latter–day Saints, The, gathering to, 79, 98, 130, 134
    power and authority in, 10, 58, 107, 115, 132, 143
Covenant, definition, 2
    born in, 35
    meal, 95–96
    See also Abrahamic covenant; Gospel covenant
Covenant people, advantages associated with, 19–20
    appointed to special service, 3, 20–22, 24
    definition, 125
    history, 39–49
    leaven of righteousness, 21–22, 48
    lose blessings through wickedness, 67
    "salt of the earth," 30
    See also Church of Jesus Christ of Latter–day Saints, The; House of Israel; Priesthood
Covenants, made when entering promised land, 46, 109
    taken out of Bible, 6, 7–8, 43
Cowdery, Oliver, ancestry, 53
    on revelation, 8

— D —

Daniel, on gospel going to all people, 120
David (king), 46, 97, 134–35
    See also Second David
Destruction, of temple, 126
    of wicked, 68, 75, 87–89, 97, 98, 130–32, 133–34

— E —

Ebal and Gerizim, 125
    blessings and cursings given, 46, 109
Eden, 1, 13, 36, 122, 124
Egypt, Israelite captivity and deliverance, 45, 71, 113, 138
Election, definition, 21
    See also Calling and election; Chosen People; Foreordination
Elias, restores keys to establish patriarchal order, 58, 61
Elijah, at Mount of Transfiguration, 56

in Kirtland Temple, 59–61
  mission and spirit of, 24, 59–61
Enoch, 53, 76
  city of, 40, 75–76
  on scattering and gathering, 109–10
  receives great vision, 81
  sees the Lord on Mount Simeon, 123
Ephraim. *See* Tribe of Ephraim.
Eternal life, promise associated with gospel covenant, 108
  to know God and Jesus Christ, 34
Eternal marriage. *See* New and everlasting covenant of marriage

— F —

Faith, and gathering of Israel, 71
  required in premortal and mortal lives, 16, 25
Faithfulness, condition for having covenants, 17, 19, 59, 126, 143–44
  See also Righteousness
Family, covenant blessings center around, 8–9, 35
  created by covenant, 35
  eternal continuation of, 8–10, 58–60
  premortal organization, 15–16
First Presidency, holds keys of gathering and building Zion, 100
  statement (1911) on gathering in native lands, 77
Foreordination, conditional, 25
  to lineage and family, 17–19
Freedom, 48, 54, 78, 142

— G —

Gathering of Israel, associated with Millennium, 97, 98–99, 129–30, 132–33
  avoiding false views on, 101
  centers in Christ, 116
  declared to Nephites, 88–89
  importance of place, 74–76
  in latter days, 143
  keys restored, 56, 58, 61, 76, 115, 116
  means of accomplishing, 70–72
  part of salvation, 87
  physical and spiritual, 71–73
  prophecies concerning, 68, 109–11
  to be accomplished by descendants of Ephraim, 55
  to build temples, 75
  to Christ and covenant people, 70–71, 88–89, 126
  to lands of inheritance, 70, 78–79, 126–27
  to receive covenants, 75, 120–21
  type of the Atonement, 80–81
  vital role of Book of Mormon in, 77–83
Gentiles, 37, 66, 75, 78, 94
  day [or times] of, 86, 96–98
  definition, 86
  House of Israel among, 80
  need to repent, 37
God, characteristics of, 35
Gospel covenant, as the Lord's acknowledgment of his people, 85
  blessings of, 8–10, 19–20, 25, 31, 40–46, 51, 60, 70–71, 79, 108–9, 126, 138–39, 143
  made in premortal life, 22–23
  meaning of "covenant" and "testament," 10
  meaning of "new and everlasting," 13–14
  responsibilities of, 3, 20–23, 24, 31–33, 35, 43, 46, 108–9
  See also Abrahamic covenant; Covenants; Priesthood

— H —

Holy Ghost, can give knowledge of remnants of Israel, 78, 94
  impact on house of Israel, 16, 19–20, 66, 73, 125, 131

promised to those who enter and keep covenants, 93
House of Israel, covenants with God upon entering promised land, 45–46
　gathering of, 69–83
　history, 39–49, 52
　in Egypt, 45
　leaven of righteousness, 21–22, 48
　ministers of salvation, 24
　scattering of, 65–69
　to be redeemed by Christ, 52
　will recognize gospel, 66
　See also Covenant people; Gathering of Israel; Scattering of Israel

— I —

Intercessory prayer, 3, 34
Isaac, 44
Isaiah, on gathering of Israel, 70–71, 110
　on gospel going to all people, 120
　on highway being cast up, 112
　on mountain of the Lord's house, 119
　on scattering of Israel, 68
Israel. *See* House of Israel

— J —

Jacob (Israel), 8, 44
　sees the Lord at Bethel, 124
Jacob (son of Lehi), on gathering of Israel, 72, 83, 127
　on coming to God, 83
　on scattering of Israel, 67, 69
Jeremiah, on Babylonian captivity, 47
　on gospel going to all people, 120
　on new covenant with Israel, 138–39
　on scattering of Israel, 66, 68
Jerusalem, 125, 127, 133
　redemption of, 86–87
　temple in, 47, 123, 126
　See also New Jerusalem

Jesus Christ, appears in Kirtland Temple, 57
　at Last Supper, 10
　baptism of, 11
　condemns unfaithful, 26
　covenants with patriarchs, 40, 44
　gives intercessory prayer, 3, 34
　gives keys of kingdom of heaven, 56
　instructs Joseph Smith, 52
　introduces new covenant to Nephites, 12, 87–98
　knows his sheep and they know his voice, 24, 66
　Mediator of New Covenant, 26
　messenger of covenant, 11
　speaks to Joseph Smith as to Abraham, 62–63
　to come suddenly to temple, 90, 98, 125
　uses metaphor of salt of the earth, 29–30, 37–38
　visits Nephites, 12, 47, 87–98
　visits ten tribes, 47, 115
　See also Second Coming of Christ; Sermon on the Mount
Jews, 47, 97, 137
　adherence to Abrahamic covenant, 37
　conversion of, 72–73, 98, 130–31
　day of, 98
　gathering of, 72–73, 75
John the Baptist, baptizes Christ, 11
　on children of Abraham, 25–26
　restores priesthood authority, 11
　role in relation to covenant, 11
　written testimony to be restored, 7
John the Revelator, and the ten tribes 111, 114, 116
　on gospel being preached to all people, 130
Joseph, significance of name, 61–62
　See also Joseph (son of Jacob); Smith, Joseph
Joseph (son of Jacob), and family, 8–9, 45

and latter-day namesake, 53–54, 61
receives birthright and blessing, 32, 45

— K —

Keys of priesthood, explanation, 56
  given to Peter, James, and John, 56
  restored, 11, 57–61
Kimball, Heber C., on Church leaders as heirs of the priesthood, 53
Kimball, Spencer W., on covenants made in premortal life, 23
  on gathering of Israel, 73–74
Kingdom of Israel, 46–47, 86
Kirtland Temple, appearance of Christ and prophets, 57–59
  dedicatory prayer, 2–3
Knowledge, of covenant with God, 7–8, 9, 31
  of God, 34, 109

— L —

Lands of inheritance, 79, 94, 116
  gathering to, 71–73, 82, 129
  may be lost, 67, 108–9
  promised to Abraham and posterity, 108–9, 125
  token of covenant, 125–26
Lathrop, John, ancestor to prominent Church leaders, 54
Law of Moses, fulfilled in Christ, 88, 93–94
Lee, Harold B., on agency and foreordination, 25
  on being loyal to royal calling, 142
  on discernment, 103–4
  on foreordination of lineage of Israel, 18–19
  on gathering in every nation, 77
Lehi, considered a Jew, 86
Life after death, includes continuation of family, 8–10
Light of Christ, 23, 30, 65–66

Lineage, affects actions, 21, 28
  and capacity to believe, 19
  does not ensure blessings, 25–27, 66
  of early Church leaders, 53–54
  of modern members of Church, 143
  premortal organization of, 15–16
Lost tribes. See Ten tribes.

— M —

McConkie, Bruce R., on baptism of Christ, 11
  on blessings received in temples, 58–59
  on conditions during Millennium, 134, 138
  on David the king, 135
  on gathering of Israel, 77, 100–101
  on gospel filling the earth, 130
  on house of Israel receiving spiritual talents, 19
  on Israel breaking covenants, 109
  on Jews accepting gospel, 73
  on physical and spiritual gathering, 72–73
  on premortal talents and development, 16–17
  on salvation through Christ, 73
  on scattering of Israel, 67
  on Second David, 136
  on temple marriage, 122
  on ten tribes, 111, 113
  on Twelve Apostles, 91
  poem about Abraham's children, 26–27
Malachi, on promises made to the fathers, 24, 59
  on the Lord coming suddenly to temple, 90, 125
Marriage, as covenant, 122
  metaphor for gospel covenant, 34
  See also New and everlasting covenant of marriage
Melchizedek, 41
Methuselah, 40

Micah, on gathering of Israel, 112
   on mountain of the Lord's house, 119
   on remnant of Jacob, 97
Millennium, 86, 96–97, 129
   conditions during, 138–39
   preparation for, 61
   time of great gathering of Israel, 98
Missionary work, assumes people recognize gospel truths, 23–24
   before and during Millennium, 130
   means of gathering Israel, 71
   responsibility of covenant people, 3, 24, 31–33, 43
   to restore memory of premortal principles, 35
Moriah, 123
Mormon, addresses Israel, 80, 110
   on house of Israel, 142
   on remnant of Joseph, 89
Moroni, appears to Joseph Smith, 24, 59
   on purposes of Book of Mormon, 31
Moses, at Sinai, 123–24
   on God's dividing inheritances to nations, 17
   prophesies of scattering and gathering, 66, 110
   restores keys to gather Israel, 56, 58, 61, 76, 115, 116, 133
   unites and delivers Israel, 45, 123–24
Mountain of the Lord's house, 119, 120–21
   See also Temple
Mutual consent, necessary part of a covenant, 8

— N —

Nelson, Russell M., on temple work, 75
   on knowing our royal lineage, 28
Nephi (son of Helaman), on scattering of Israel, 67
Nephi (son of Lehi), on Book of Mormon, 79–80
   on Christ's baptism, 11
   on destruction of wicked 131–32
   on gathering of Israel, 71–72, 126
   on loss of plain and precious things, 5
   on Millennium, 132
   on repentance, 27
   on scattering of tribes of Israel, 47, 68–69
New and everlasting covenant, explanation, 12–14
New and everlasting covenant of marriage, 58, 60
   ensures eternal continuation of family, 9
   in Abraham's family, 42–45
   in temples, 122
   power and authority to perform, 10
New Jerusalem, 52, 91, 98, 133
Noah, 40

— O —

Olive tree allegory, 27–28, 71, 82, 137

— P —

Packer, Boyd K., on keeping covenants, 36–37
   on premortal life, 15
Palestine, 72–73, 125
Passover, Elijah returns during, 59
Patriarch, office of, 18, 39–40
Patriarchal order, keys restored, 58
   the Lord's system of government, 39–41
Patriots, American, 48, 54
Paul, on all being one in Christ, 137
   on God's setting times and bounds, 17–18
   on premortal declaration of gospel principles, 22
   on seed of Abraham, 27
   on working out salvation, 35
Peter, 7, 56
Pratt, Parley P., on duties of Israel, 23

on lineage, 53
on staying true to Abrahamic covenant, 37
poem on restoration of gospel, 63–64
Premortal life, 66
covenants made during, 14, 22–24
gospel principles taught during, 22, 35
lineages and families organized during, 15–16
preparation during, 33
tied to mortal life, 16–18
Priesthood, authority restored, 11, 51, 56–61
Early Church leaders heirs to, 53–54
in Millennium, 138
necessary in order to have covenants, 8
received by ancient patriarchs, 39–41
to be carried to nations through Abraham's descendants, 21–22, 31–32, 43
See also Gospel covenant; Keys of priesthood
Promised land, for modern house of Israel, 51, 125
gathering to, 70
Israelites in, 46–47, 109
token of covenant, 126
Prophets, 8, 9, 33, 35, 37, 51, 79, 113

— Q —

Quorum of Twelve, 55, 91
holds vital keys, 91–92
Nephite, 12, 90–91
sustaining of, 91–92
symbolic representation of twelve tribes, 91–92, 99–100
to direct gathering of Israel and building of Zion, 99–100

— R —

Redemption, in latter days, 13, 52, 113

Remnant of Jacob [or Joseph], among Gentiles, 97
among Nephites, 89, 94
definition, 86
promises to, 78, 99
Repentance, 27, 65, 83, 89
Restoration of gospel, fulfills God's promise to Enoch, 81
fulfills God's promises to Abraham, 51
includes restoration of Abrahamic covenant, 63
reestablishes kingdom of God on earth, 55–56
Revelation, 8–10, 31, 141
Righteousness, 109, 122, 132
Christ's example, 11
condition of receiving blessings, 20–24
in premortal life, 17
of Abraham and posterity, 42, 48

— S —

Sacrament, among Nephites, 95
Sacrifice, Abraham's, 26, 123
definition, 121–22
new and old forms, 88
in temples, 122
Salt, imagery associated with making covenants, 29–30, 37–38
Salvation, centers in Christ and covenants, 2–3, 13, 31–32, 34–37
and work of gathering, 70
Salvation of our God, definition, 87
Sarah, 42, 123
Saviors on Mount Zion, 24, 38, 62, 142
Scattering of Israel, 13, 46–47
reasons for, 65–69, 109
Sealing, 21
binds families together, 59–61, 122
keys of, 56–61
to Abrahamic covenant, 75
Second Coming of Christ, 129–30, 133, 134

foreshadowed in 3 Nephi, 98–99
response of Jews, 131
Second David, 134–36
Sermon on the Mount, 12, 30, 91–94
Service, 2–3, 38
See also Missionary work; Priesthood
Seth, 40
Shem, 40–41
Simeon, Mount, 123
Sinai, Mount, 123–24
Smith, Hyrum, among noble ones in premortal life, 33
Smith, Joseph, among noble ones in premortal life, 33
   chosen lineage, 52–53, 55
   covenant of salvation restored to, 9
   instructed to gather Israel, 52, 111, 115
   Kirtland Temple dedicatory prayer, 2
   modern Abraham, 61–63
   on beginning of fulfillment of gospel covenant, 61
   on Christian martyrs, 48
   on city of righteousness, 75–76
   on David the king, 134
   on family organization in heaven, 16
   on gathering, 69–70, 75, 115
   on gospel being taken to all people, 120
   on impact of Holy Ghost on descendants of Abraham, 16, 19–20
   on Israel receiving priesthood, 62
   on loss of clarity in Bible, 6
   on Millennium, 133
   on mission of Elijah, 60
   on Nephite Apostles, 92
   on temples, 75
   on Zion, 82
   patriarchal blessing, 62
   poem on rejecting gospel covenant, 144
   restored doctrine of premortal life, 15
   transformation in Kirtland Temple, 57

Smith, Joseph F., vision on redemption of the dead, 33
Smith, Joseph Fielding, on agency and keeping commandments, 23
   on purposes for scattering of Israel, 69
Smith, Joseph, Sr., gives patriarchal blessing to Joseph Smith, Jr., 62
Snow, Erastus, on accomplishments of chosen people, 141–42
Snow, Lorenzo, ancestry, 54
   on covenants made in premortal life, 22
Spirit of the Lord. See Holy Ghost

— T —

Talents, spiritual, 16–17, 19, 25
Taylor, John, among noble ones in premortal life, 33
   on the Millennium, 136
Temple, in land Bountiful, 89, 125
   in Jerusalem, 47, 123, 126
   "mountain of the Lord's house," 121
   place of covenant, 8–9, 121
   purposes of, 127
   Savior to come suddenly to, 90, 98, 125
Temple work, 10, 58–61, 62, 75
   foundations laid in premortal life, 33
   part of gathering of Israel, 70, 71
Temples, 10, 124
   gathering of Israel is to build, 75
   means of receiving promises given to fathers, 60
Ten tribes, 37, 46–47
   location of, 104–8, 109–10
   visited by Christ, 47, 115
Times of the Gentiles, definition, 86
Top, Brent, on foreordination of groups, 17
Transfiguration, 7, 57
Tribe of Ephraim, 47, 53, 111
   blessings and responsibilities, 32–33
   membership does not ensure blessings, 25–26

purposes for scattering of, 69
responsible for gathering of Israel, 56, 110
"soldiers of God," 48
Tribes of Israel, 45–47, 56, 62, 80, 133

— U —

United States, 48, 76, 97–98

— W —

Wentworth letter, 61
Whitney, Orson F., on American patriots, 48–49
  poem on souls chosen by God, 20
Widtsoe, John A., on premortal life, 24
Woodruff, Wilford, among noble ones in premortal life, 33
  on children of Israel recognizing gospel, 66
  on Ephraimite lineage, 53
  on signers of Declaration of Independence, 49
Worthiness. *See* Righteousness

— Y —

Young, Brigham, among noble ones in premortal life, 33
  ancestry, 54
  instructed by Joseph Smith, 16
  on gathering, 74
  on Joseph Smith, 53, 62
  on lineage of Church leaders, 53–54
  on serving God in any location, 76

— Z —

Zenos. *See* Olive tree allegory
Zion, 116, 119
  gathered from all nations, 77
  in America, 76, 98
  place of gathering of righteous, 56, 70, 74–77, 82
  Quorum of Twelve to direct building of, 99–100
  redemption of, 52, 112–13
  to return to earth in last days, 40